THE HISTORY OF THE ROBINSON FAMILY

Volume II

The Burnett, Springer, Kennedy, McDougal and Larrimer Ancestral Lines of the Robinson Family In America

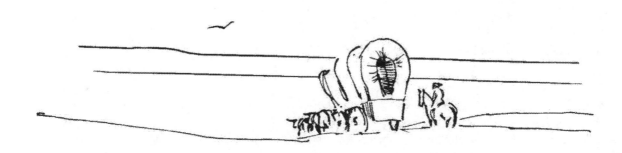

by
Franklin Willard Robinson, Jr.

2007

www.trafford.com
North America & international
toll-free: 844-688-6899 (USA & Canada)
fax: 812 355 4082

TABLE OF CONTENTS

<u>Section Title</u>   **<u>Page No.</u>**

ACKNOWLEDGMENTS

Acknowledgment for support and help in the preparation of this family history is given to:

- Joan Robinson, my wife, who traveled many miles with me over the paths of discovery. Without her love, encouragement, and support many of these stories would never have been recovered.

- Gail Robinson Van Camp, my daughter, who has encouraged me to complete the project, and has faithfully helped me with the editing of the stories, and computer enhanced several of the historic pictures included.

- Don Dutcher, my friend, who has given years to take me through the perilous paths of computer writing, picture enhancing, book formatting and editing. Without his invaluable involvement, there never would have been this family history.

- Louise Holler Craddock, my long lost cousin, and her husband Sheldon Craddock. Their invaluable genealogical research provided the "key" to unlocking the long-lost ancestral lines of the Robinson family.

- Dean Estes, my friend and talented artist who crafted the ceramic tile shown on this book cover. His creation depicts the Robinson family as they began their covered wagon journey to California in 1859.

FOREWORD

The Burnett, Springer, Kennedy, McDougal & Larrimer Ancestral Lines of the Robinson Family in America

Much of the history of the Robinson family has been carried down from generation to generation through the stories that have been told from parents to children. This can be helpful, but inaccuracies and gaps in these histories presented a challenge. This was especially true in pursuing the last years of the Wesley Burnett line and the early years of the McDougal and Kennedy lines of the family. Following are the incidents and events that finally enabled a more complete story of these amazing families.

My father, Franklin W. Robinson, told many stories of the time he spent his summer vacations on his grandfather's Corral de Los Mulos Rancho at Adelaida, which was 12 miles west of Paso Robles, California. There he cut tan bark that was used to tan the cattle hides for the market. They were happy and eventful years for my father.

I have memories, too, of when I was a very young child and often visited my great aunt, Helen Burnett Borton, in Long Beach. She was a younger sister of my grandmother Rosamond Burnett Robinson. I never met my grandmother, Rosamond Burnett Robinson, because she died in her Long Beach home in 1918, a month before I was born.

My great uncle, J.K. Burnett ("Uncle Bud"), I met twice. He is the only Burnett with whom I actually conversed. Both meetings with him made a lasting impression. The first was when I was seven years old. Uncle Bud visited our old Corona del Valle Ranch. While he was there, he told me many stories about his early life on the California frontier. Among other things, he told me he was two years younger than my grandmother, Rosa. "Your grandmother Rosa and I were both born in the same log cabin on the Nacimiento River near Paso Robles," he said.

The second time I met Uncle Bud, it was eighteen years later, September of 1944, in Paso Robles, California. This was during World War II. I had been released from the Long Beach Naval Hospital and was to depart from San Francisco to serve a second tour of duty as a bomber pilot on the aircraft carrier *U.S.S. Suwanee,* somewhere north of New Guinea. I found my Uncle Bud on his death bed. He was eighty-three years old. It was an emotional visit. He was anxious to review the events of his life and the pioneering days of his illustrious parents.

"They were the founders of much of this beautiful land, from Paso Robles to the coast north of Cayucos. There is a rich history here," he told me. For the next couple of hours, speaking with a resonance in his voice, even as his body was failing, he reviewed many of the highlights of the family history. He communicated with clarity and I marveled at his amazing mind. I wanted to learn more.

Thirty-four years later, while going through the desk of my father, who had died in Long Beach, California, in 1978, I found a forty-eight-page manuscript written by Uncle Bud. On faded onionskin paper, which had deteriorated over the years, he had written the story of the early years of his father's life. It was entitled, "Incidents in the Life of Wesley Burnett." Here was a goldmine of early California history. To my knowledge, this was the only manuscript of this family history still in existence, without which this fascinating story would have been lost. The problem was that J.K Burnett's document ended in the 1870's, while the family was still living on the Cayucos Ranch. Too, we had little knowledge of my great grandmother, her early life, or of the circumstances of her death. The search would go on.

In 1993, after twelve years of research, I published the book, <u>The History of the Robinson Family</u>. During the following twelve years, I experienced some frustration because I had never been able to establish important aspects of the illustrious lives of my great grandfather, Wesley Burnett, and his mother, Mary Springer Burnett. I also knew very little of the early life of my great grandmother, Mary Kennedy Burnett, other than that she had made the trip in covered wagon to California with her family in 1852.

For these reasons, in 1994, my wife Joan and I made a trip to San Louis Obispo County in California to see if we could unearth more information on these branches of our family history. We stayed in a pleasant motel in Cayucos, a couple miles south of the old Geronimo Grant, which Wesley Burnett had purchased from San Juan Castro prior to the Civil War. This spectacular ranch, which included several miles of still undeveloped land along the coast north of Cayucos, was my Grandmother Robinson's home during her childhood years.

While in Cayucos, I strolled out on the old pier. My thoughts went back to those colorful days when my great grandfather, Wesley Burnett, watched an occasional ship dock to take away the wool and grain. I stopped and chatted with an elderly Portuguese resident who was fishing from the pier.

"My family settled on this beautiful coastline several generations ago," he said. We shared our ancestral roots.

"Why don't you check an old pioneer cemetery in the back country," he volunteered. "You might find the resting place of your great grandparents. Take the old canyon road up back of town until you reach Highway 46, and then go on east for a few miles until you see a road that takes you north to a little way place called Adelaida. You'll find someone who can direct you to the old cemetery where many of those early pioneers are buried."

"Thank you," I said to the helpful fisherman. "There is no information on my ancestors' deaths in the county records, so we will follow your suggestion."

Not being familiar with the area, Joan and I drove to a ranch house near the general area to which we had been directed. A pleasant lady answered the door. "Well," she said, in answer to our inquiry, "you are on the right road. Just go another mile and you will see the cemetery on your right. The gate is locked, but I'll give you a key. Bring it back when you finish your visit."

We drove down the mountain road, a road laced on each side with live oaks, chaparral, and scattered pines. We located the old cemetery, opened the gate, and began our search. It was with disappointment that we left without locating the Burnett family burial plots. The lady at the ranch house shared our disappointment, when we returned to give her the key to the cemetery. "You know," she said. "There is a man named MacGillivray who lives a couple of miles from here. He is an historian who recently finished a book about this area. He might be able to help you."

In a few minutes we located an old restored 19th century ranch house, fronted by a broad lawn, bordered by lilacs and flowering bulb plants, and shaded by a giant white oak. A spacious covered porch gave protected entrance to the delightful home. I knocked on the screen door.

J. Fraser MacGillivray, 8910 Adelaida Road, Paso Robles, California, greeted us. He was genuinely interested when I introduced myself as the great grandson of Wesley Burnett. "I was looking for the grave site of my great grandparents," I said.

"You have come to the right place," he answered. "When you went to the cemetery, you didn't look high enough. The Burnett plot is on the ridge overlooking the main cemetery. A marble pillar marks Mary Burnett's grave. Wesley is buried beside her in an unmarked grave." MacGillivray continued, "Wesley Burnett gave the cemetery property to Adelaida after his wife's death in 1878. She was the first to be buried there. Wesley was living on the old Rancho Corral de los Mulos. He could sit on his front porch, look across the road, and on up to the ridge to where his beloved Mary was buried."

Fraser MacGillivray continued with his story. "I just finished a book on the history of Adelaida. You will find Wesley Burnett mentioned more times in the book than any other of the original pioneers. You might want to contact Louise Holler Craddock, a great granddaughter of Wesley Burnett. She was very helpful, as she had done extensive work on the history of this pioneer family. She lives at Lake Tahoe on the Nevada side. I understand Louise and Sheldon Craddock plan to have a maker placed on Wesley Burnett's grave."

Joan and I thanked Fraser MacGillivray for his valuable help. Later we located the peaceful tree-shaded Burnett burial sites on the high ridge above the main cemetery.

We appreciatively report that the graves of these intrepid, beloved and historic ancestors are now appropriately marked—this through generosity of Louise and Sheldon Craddock. Too, we are sad to report that a year after our visit with Fraser MacGillivary, we received word of his death. Our family will be forever indebted to him for his historic research.

*   *   *

I had never met Louise Holler Craddock, but I did remember her father, Wesley Holler. He was my father's first cousin. In the early 1920's, Wesley Holler visited us on the old Corona del Valle Ranch in northern Los Angeles County. I did follow the lead given me by Fraser MacGillivray, and soon established contact with my long lost cousin. I mention this in some detail, because Louise Holler Craddock became the key to finishing the Burnett story and the completion of this book, The Robinson Family History (Vol. 2), through the lineage of the Burnett, Springer, Kennedy and McDougal families. The full history of these ancestors had eluded us over the years. I value Sheldon and Louise Craddock, not only because of the common family history we share, but because of the friendship we have established through our mutual search for the added details of our family history.

F. Willard Robinson, 2007

THE KENNEDY FAMILY IN AMERICA

Foundations in Scotland, 1800

Immigration to Canada, 1825-1830

Immigration to Illinois, USA, 1842

Wagon Train to California, 1852

Pioneer Days, San Luis Obispo County, California, 1859

INTRODUCTION TO THE MARY KENNEDY FAMILY IN AMERICA

My paternal great-grandmother was Mary Kennedy. She was a young widow living in Santa Cruz, California with her two young boys. It was there that she met and married Wesley Burnett on June 4, 1860. I knew she had come to California by ox-team with her family in 1852. But beyond this, establishing the details of the Kennedy family history has been elusive. For the past twenty-five years, much of the life of Mary Kennedy Burnett could not be definitely determined. I knew little of her early life, the story of her parents, the details of her death, nor her place of burial. Through the persistent genealogical work of Louise Craddock, great-granddaughter of Mary Burnett, and her husband Sheldon Craddock, Mary Kennedy's lineage can now be recorded with accuracy.

The introduction to the histories of the Burnett, Springer, Kennedy, and McDougal families in America, tells of the fascinating series of events, which now make it possible to record this history—a brave and adventurous family who sailed the Atlantic to Canada, established a frontier life in Illinois for ten years, and then spanned the continent in a covered wagon pulled by a team of oxen.

Later Mary Kennedy, my great-grandmother, raised a family and helped pioneer a spectacular inland and coastal wilderness in the central California area, from Paso Robles to Cayucos. We now can look back on her forty-eight years of life with wonder, gratitude, and appreciation.

F. Willard Robinson
2005

RELATIONSHIP OF THE
FRANKLIN W. ROBINSON FAMILY
TO THE MARY KENNEDY FAMILY LINEAGE

Robert Kennedy   ←   **Ann Philip**

Aberdeen, Scotland   (marriage)   Christened, Renfrew, Scotland 1808
(<u>descendants</u>)

↓

James Kennedy   ←   **Helen McDougal**

Christened, Aberdeen, Scotland 1801   Christened, Renfrew, Scotland 1808
d. San Jose, California 1886   d. San Jose, California 1886

Mary Kennedy Cooper   ←   **Wesley Burnett**

b. Canada 1830   b. New Lebanon, Indiana 1818
d. Adelaida, California 1878   d. Adelaida, California 1905

Rosamond Robinson   ←   **John Wesley Robinson**

b. Nacimiento, California 1863   b. Monroe Co., Iowa 1855
d. Long Beach, California 1918   d. Berkeley, California 1936

Franklin W. Robinson   ←   **Hope Gould**

b. Grangeville, California 1859   b. Monterey, California 1893
d. Long Beach, California 1978   d. Long Beach, California 1958

JAMES AND HELEN McDOUGAL KENNEDY
(First Kennedys in America – 1820s)

James Kennedy was born in Old Machar, Aberdeen, Scotland in 1801. He was christened in Aberdeen on July 6, 1801. His parents were Robert and Anne Philip Kennedy. This record is confirmed in the Scottish Church Record Index.

Aberdeen is a port city on the northeast coast of Scotland, known for its maritime economy, beautiful landscapes and historic castles. It has a rich protestant religious history. Scotland is where, in 1611, the King James Version of the Bible was written. Unfortunately, a century of religious upheaval followed. In 1618, Catholic Emperor Ferdinand II had decided to eradicate Protestantism entirely. This resulted in the Thirty Year War that left millions dead. Following this dark time in history, "The Age of Reason" emerged, and with it the growth of the Free Church movement. This resulted in another time of religious instability. It is apparent from the records that the Kennedy family was deeply involved in the Protestant movement, but their desire for freedom and economic opportunity would propel this adventurous and courageous young couple, via Canada, to America and the American dream.

Records would indicate that James Kennedy married Helen McDougal, a girl who lived with her parents in Greenock, Renfrew, Scotland, some twenty miles west of Glasgow. Helen was born January 18, 1808. She was the daughter of John McDougall and Elizabeth McKellar, who were married in Greenock, Scotland on May 31, 1805. Elizabeth Keller's parents were Daniel McKellar and Janet Leitch. Elizabeth was christened in Greenock on August 29, 1784. This, then, is four generations of the Helen McDougall Kennedy family identified as living in Greenock, Scotland. We can only imagine the wrench to these old stable families when James and now Helen McDougal Kennedy, embarked into the unknown of a new world far across the Atlantic.

The date of their marriage is not known. We can only surmise that it was prior to embarking for Canada and their landing in Nova Scotia. This being correct, it would be fair to give their ages at the time of their marriage in Scotland as, James 18, and Helen 15. This courageous young couple then departed for Canada sometime after 1825, but before 1830. Mary Kennedy (Burnett), their first child, was born somewhere in eastern Canada.

James and Helen raised nine children, six of whom were born in Canada by 1841, and three more in Illinois, before they left for California in 1852. We can write this with assurance because records indicate that they established a little frontier farm in Newport, Lake County, Illinois. Newport is not on our modern day maps, so undoubtedly it was then a small community of settlers who sought good land and mutual support near Cedar Lake, some thirty miles southeast of Chicago. It is amazing; this venerable couple raised a family of nine children, all who lived to gain productive lives without a death in the immediate family—and all on frontiers, where life at it its best was tenuous.

These are the children of James and Helen Kennedy:

- Mary (the oldest and our direct ancestor) B. 1830 in Canada. M. Wesley Burnett in 1860. She was the widow of Alexander Cooper.
- Robert D., b. 1832, in Canada, d. April 8, 1880 at age 48 and buried at Oak Hill Cemetery in San Jose. He was probably unmarried. Robert D. Kennedy served with the Union Army in the Civil War.
- Elizabeth, b. about 182, in Canada, m. a man by the name of Boyle . She was not in the 1860 census at McCartysville, California.
- William W., b. 1837, in Canada. 1860 census record for McCartysville shows that he was a school teacher. He lived in Fossil, Oregon in 1886.
- John M., b. 1839, in Canada. d. Stockton, California, January 2, 1909
- Jeanette, b. 184, in Canada, m. a man by the name of Malcolm. Lived in Watsonville, California
- James G., b. 1843, in Illinois. He was at one time the principal and superintendent of Polytechnic High School in San Francisco.
- Margaret E., b. 1847, in Illinois, M. a man by the name of Wild. She is buried at Oak Hill Cemetery.
- Thomas E., b. 1852, in Illinois. d. San Francisco, March 29, 1893. Buried at Oak Hill Cemetery. From his grave marker it appears that he was married to a Margaret M. Kennedy, who died in 1896 at age fifty-five.

In 1852, James Kennedy and his wife Helen, with their nine children ranging in age from one to twenty-two (Mary, our direct ancestor was the oldest), loaded their ox-drawn wagons and left their land in Newport, Lake County, Illinois. We do not know the exact time of the family's departure, but we do know that it was later than March 16, 1852. We know this because James Kennedy received his naturalization papers on that date. He was now a citizen of the United States of America. "Oh happy day," for this courageous family!

One cannot be certain as to where the Kennedy family eventually organized their wagon train, as they started out over the vast prairie on the trail to the West. There were several jumping-off sites along the Missouri River where the wagon trains were "formed up" for the adventurous journey ahead. The California/Oregon trail system was developed over a period of several years and numerous alternate routes were tried. A quarter of a million people traveled the route west during the 1840's and 1850's. Each wagon train sought the best as far as terrain, length and sufficient water and grass for livestock was concerned.

However, most of these routes merged at Ash Hollow, a woodsy glen on the Nebraska side of the Platte River. The meadow was lined with wild roses and shaded by majestic ash. The various wild flowers, blooming in profusion when the spring travelers arrived at Ash Hollow, added fragrance to the fresh air. A series of cool streams rippled and undulated until their happy song was merged in the translucent pond near the center of the verdant hollow. It was the perfect place of respite for the Kennedy family, before toiling again over the challenging trail ahead. The young people romped in the grass, and washed the mud and dust from their belongings. It was a good time also to remove the wheels from the wagons and lubricate the axles with tar and tallow for the difficult pull ahead. With their stock rested and their wagon ready, they again took up the trail that followed westward along the sandy banks of the North Platte River.

The uphill grade through this stretch of the route was slight, but constant. Even in June the nights grew steadily colder because of the rising altitude. Far off on the horizon rose the snow-patched Laramie Mountains, forming stepping stones to the Rockies.

Now, at various points beside the trail, strange formations of earth and rock protruded to the sky. They watched with great interest as they passed these massive natural monuments: Court House Rock, Chimney Rock, and Scott's Bluff. Deeper and deeper the wagons moved into the central highlands, and soon a landmark came in sight that they had been anticipating for several weeks. It was originally one of the posts established by the American Fur Company for the fur trade. Now the turreted and picketed rampart at Fort Laramie was primarily a station for the cavalry troops of the United States government.

The Kennedys shivered in the early July nights and mornings along the trail, as they approached South Pass and the Continental Divide. At a place called Ice Slough, seventy miles west of Independence Rock, a bed of ice lay about a foot underneath the sod. In the heat of the day, James Kennedy stopped the wagons and had his children chop out big chunks of ice for their water casks. The presence of ice verified that they had climbed to considerable altitude, actually about 7,000 feet, as they reached the rolling approach to South Pass, key to the West. Here the trail crossed the Continental Divide, then dipped toward the Pacific basin for the first time.

The stalwart travelers, having crossed the central ridge of the continent, bumped on over the rocks to the first major water crossing in Wyoming at Green River. The place was marked by a butte of singular formation, like a ruined edifice with a majestic dome buttressed by rock pillars. The Green River was the swiftest and deepest river they had to cross on the entire trip. The wagons were ferried across on large rafts. The men drove the loose stock into the water, forcing them to swim through the earth-colored current from spring runoff to the far side. It was a passage of peril; a formative barrier to the intrepid immigrants seeking new life in the western regions of the continent.

Fifty miles beyond Soda Springs was Fort Hall, a short distance north of present day Pocatello, Idaho. Here the wagons prepared to split up, a few miles west of Fort Hall, fording at the Raft River. The trail to California branched off the main Oregon Trail. It was a sad time for all the people on the wagon trains, because the travelers had often developed close relationships on their long passage from the Missouri River. Now for many, they would never see their special friends again.

The Kennedy family continued with those who chose to make California their new home. On they passed through the City of Rocks, near present day Burley, Idaho, and through the Nevada Mountains until they reached the upper level of the Humboldt Plain. The Humboldt River, which lies entirely within the Great Basin of the country, has no connection with the sea. It takes a general course westward along what is now Interstate Highway 80, meandering by the now-established towns of Elko, Winnemucca, and Lovelock, Nevada. There the waning river dies in the alkaline waste of the Humboldt Sink. Here the weary immigrants urged their spent stock through a desert furnace in the final effort to reach the great Sierra barrier, and then the fertile inland California valleys of the Sacramento. James and Helen Kennedy, along with their nine children, ranging in age from twenty-two years to one-year, successfully completed the journey.

The vicissitudes through which this family passed, the perils they endured, along with others who made this two-thousand-mile trip through the wilderness, are without precedent in history. They passed through hostile Indian country, crossed two mountain chains equal to the Alps, mucked through miles of mud, forded treacherous rivers, and endured tracts of burning desert. It is a story of heroism, of daring and of sublime endurance.

*   *   *

The genealogical record, discovered through the work of Sheldon and Louise Craddock, records, "It seems likely that the Kennedy's traveled to California with a Cooper family, because their daughter Mary married Alexander Cooper in Sacramento on February 13, 1853."

From the information I have been able to glean, I am convinced that the relationship between Mary Kennedy and Alexander Cooper did develop on their 1852 journey over the trail to California.

In the History of Adelaida, the author, Fraser MacGillivray, writes, "Mary Kennedy Burnett had come to California with the Cooper family. The Kennedys and the Coopers worked unsuccessfully for a while as miners in the Sacramento and Feather River gold fields. The families experienced great tragedy when, sometime after May 1855, Mary's husband Alexander Cooper, mysteriously disappeared and was declared dead."

This loss of Alexander Cooper left Mary a widow with two small boys. The details of her future with Wesley Burnett are told in the story of Mary Kennedy Burnett. We do know that Mary and her two small children moved with the Kennedy family to McCartysville (now Saratoga) in Santa Clara County sometime before 1860. James Kennedy is listed in the historical records as a tollgate keeper.

There were two toll roads out of Saratoga into the magnificent redwood forests of the Santa Cruz Mountains. James Kennedy served as the tollgate keeper on the much grander toll road known as the Saratoga and Pescadero Turnpike, which was started in 1865 and completed in 1871. The northern slopes of the Santa Cruz Mountains had been denuded of suitable redwood trees and the road was constructed to bring redwood logs from the southern slope of the mountains to the lumber mills at Saratoga. The road ran from Saratoga, following the route of the present-day Highway 9, to the summit at the boundary between Santa Clara County and Santa Cruz County. The first one-and-a-half miles of the road follow Big Basin Way and the next five-and-a-half miles follow the Congress Springs Road. The road went down the route of Highway 9, past the vicinity of the headwaters of Pescadero Creek and the San Lorenzo River, which was an area of rich redwood forests. Today this general area can be identified on a map by the names Waterman Gap, Saratoga Toll Road, and San Lorenzo Park.

The road then continued down through the San Lorenzo Valley to the town of Boulder Creek near Mount Herman. The location of the two tollgates is unknown, but it is obvious James Kennedy was the tollgate keeper on the north side of the Santa Cruz Mountains somewhere near Saratoga.

Sometime before 1880, James and Helen Kennedy moved to San Jose. As happens in healthy families, the children had married and left to make lives of their own. Their widowed daughter, Mary, caught the eye of a well-to-do rancher and sawmill owner on Soquel creek named Wesley Burnett. Wesley sold his sawmill and ranch holdings in the Santa Clara Valley in 1859. He married Mary Kennedy (Cooper), and took her and her two boys, Charles and John, to establish a cattle ranch enterprise on the Nacimiento River in northern San Luis Obispo County.

It was a lonely time for the Kennedys, for over the years they had depended on their oldest daughter to bring added stability to their large family. Now they were not only losing their beloved daughter to a new frontier, but the two grandsons that had depended on them for much love after the tragic loss of their father, Alexander Cooper. The collected diaries I have reviewed, note that from time to time, when loneliness became too great, either the mother Helen, or daughter Mary, would make the long four-day trip by stage coach and wagon from San Jose to the Burnett ranches, depending upon which ranch the Burnetts were living on at the time. Any given trip might have been to the original homestead on the Nacimiento, or later to Adelaida, to Villa Creek, or to the Geronimo Grant just north of Cayucos.

None of these journeys were easy in those early days. Sadly, the visits ended when Mary was taken by death in 1878, eight years before her parents died in San Jose during 1886. We know little of the other eight children of James and Helen Kennedy, with the exception of their seventh child, James G. Kennedy. Information obtained from the 1892 edition of The Californian Illustrated Magazine in San Francisco is worth noting:

James G. Kennedy, the principal of the Franklin school, is an experienced and successful educator and one of the best exponents of advanced methods in the San Francisco School Department. He is forty-nine years of age, a native of Illinois, and in 1842, came across the plains to California with an ox team. He was a graduate of Santa Clara College. He taught at various times in all grades of high school. The schools of San Jose and Santa Clara County attained a high degree of proficiency under his able administration as Superintendent. Since he entered the San Francisco School Department, Mr.

Kennedy has been an active and enthusiastic advocate of the "New Education." As Head Inspecting Teacher, during the administration of Superintendent Anderson, he was instrumental in raising the scholastic standard of the San Francisco Schools, into which he introduced many new and improved methods of teaching. Mr. Kennedy planned, organized and conducted successfully, the Cogswell Polytechnic College, from which he voluntarily resigned to head the Franklin High School.

James and Helen Kennedy were living in San Jose on Tenth Street when James died, March 30, 1886, at the age of 81. Eight-and-a-half months later, December 18, 1886, at the age of 78, Helen McDougal Kennedy joined her husband in death. These venerable and courageous ancestors are buried at Oak Hill Memorial Cemetery in San Jose, California.

OAK HILL MEMORIAL PARK
100 Curtner Avenue
San Jose, California

Photo courtesy of Sheldon and Louise Craddock
Enlarged and computer-enhanced by Don Dutcher
James Kennedy: Lot 1, Block 83. Sec I, Grave 4
Helen Kennedy: Lot 1, Block 83. Sec 1. Grave 3

PARENTS OF MARY KENNEDY BURNETT

James Kennedy
1801 – 1886

Helen McDougal Kennedy
1808–1886

In their youth, the desire for freedom and economic opportunity propelled this adventurous and courageous couple to America and the American Dream.

MARY KENNEDY BURNETT
1830 – 1878

The early years in the life of Mary Kennedy Burnett are covered in the account of her parents, James and Helen Kennedy. We know that she was born in eastern Canada in 1830, and then moved early in her life with her parents to Toronto, Canada. Mary was the oldest of nine children, six of whom were born in Canada. Three other siblings were born in Illinois between 1843 and early 1852. We also know that the family established a family farm near Newport, Lake County, Illinois. As soon as her father, James Kennedy, received his naturalization papers, on March 16, 1852, they loaded the family wagons and started the perilous journey across the continent for California. They made the trip, as described in her parents' account, without major incident. It was a feat of quiet valor, especially when one realizes that the nine children ranged in age from twenty-one-year-old Mary, to Thomas, a newborn. Mary shouldered major responsibility for the family during the four to five-month passage. It was a worthy apprenticeship for the heroic pioneer life ahead for Mary, who was a feminine and beautiful young lady.

*   *   *

The story of Mary's first husband, Alexander Cooper, has been an elusive one in family history. After gleaning through the various accounts, which have filtered down over the years, the following appears to be accurate.

The members of the Cooper family were friends of the Kennedy family and they traveled together in separate wagons, as the caravan moved west in the late spring of 1852. Alexander Cooper was a handsome and ambitious young man who, as an older son in the Cooper family assumed major responsibilities

15

for the stock, teams, and wagons as the families toiled west. It was natural that Mary Kennedy and Alexander Cooper would develop a romantic attraction.

When the families arrived in Sacramento, in the late summer of 1852, the men of both families headed for the Feather River gold fields. The first year they did not have success in mining for gold. In the early fall of 1852, before the snow fell in the Sierra, they returned to Sacramento. There on February 13, 1853, Mary and Alexander were married. As the winter snows in the lower Sierra melted, Mary and Alexander Cooper pitched camp at Placerville. Here in this mining camp, some forty miles east of Sacramento, Mary gave birth, in November 1853, to her first son, John Cooper.

During this time Alexander continued his search for gold in the creeks above Placerville. Apparently he experienced some success, for it is evident that sometime between 1853 and 1854, the new family built up enough resources to purchase a beautiful tract of land at San Juan Bautista, some twenty miles north of Salinas, California. It was in San Juan Bautista where Mary and Alexander's second son, Charles Richard Cooper, was born in May of 1856.

San Juan Bautista was a particularly fertile area of the state and records indicate Alexander developed a herd of "fancy" livestock, worth considerable money. One day he missed a number of his prized cattle. He saddled his horse and went out to look for them. Great tragedy struck the family! Alexander Cooper disappeared. All presumed that he had fallen victim to the cattle thieves that roamed the lawless land at the time. No one ever knew what happened for certain, but he was never seen or heard from again.

Later, Alexander Cooper was declared officially dead, leaving Mary a widow with two young sons. In her despair, she and the children returned by team and wagon to her parents' home in McCartysville (now Saratoga) in Santa Clara County. In this shattering time of sorrow and readjustment, Mary, with intrepid courage, began a new life as a teacher in Santa Cruz, California.

*   *   *

During this time, settlers often got together for community picnics. On one of these occasions, a sawmill owner, Wesley Burnett from Soquel, attended. Soquel was some ten miles west of Santa Cruz   Wesley's eyes soon fell on Mary Kennedy Cooper. He was smitten! Mary was dressed in a showy dress of pale pink and light plaid, which complemented her brown hair and fair complexion. Wesley turned to his companions, "Boys, there is my future wife!"

Mary Kennedy Cooper and Wesley Burnett were married shortly after, on June 4, 1860, in Santa Clara County. This began a new chapter in Mary's life. It would be one of heroic challenge, hardship, and pioneer adventure. Her new husband, Wesley, had a heart for life on the new frontier. It had been bred into his genes. Now he would establish a cattle operation on open land in northern San Luis Obispo County on the Nacimiento River. This is where Wesley Burnett took Mary and her two sons to establish the new family. Their home was built on the south side of the Nacimiento River about four miles west of where it's joined by the Las Tablos. (Today most of this area is under water, due to a dam that was built many years later on the Nacimiento River).

A log cabin was constructed. It had a fireplace built of cobble stones from the river and they dug a well. A barn and corrals, also built of logs, were erected. Several hundred head of cattle were purchased and placed on the range adjoining the house. No land was purchased or owned. The land was all open government range. If any one wished to establish a ranch on the Nacimiento, all a family needed to do was to find an unoccupied place where there was water available. They would build a cabin and corrals with the logs that were available on the property, and then call it their ranch.

The first two families to settle in this area of San Luis Obispo County were the James Lynch family, in 1859, and the Wesley Burnett family, in 1860. This area later became known as Adelaida. Its history was recorded by J. Fraser MacGillivray in his book, History of Adelaida, California (1992). In this extensive history, Wesley Burnett and Mary Kennedy Burnett are mentioned more times than any other pioneers in northern San Luis Obispo County. This book, along with the Incidents in the Life of Wesley Burnett, written in 1932 by their son, J. K. Burnett, has been a valued resource in preparing this history. It is from these sources that we now have valued glimpses into the life of Mary Kennedy Burnett. Following are vignettes from these histories, which describe the difficult life of the early pioneer women of the Nacimiento.

Mary Kennedy Burnett's neighbor, while living on the Nacimiento, was Alice Lynch who lived five miles up and across the river. In her diary she reported:

In the year before Mary Kennedy arrived I could go a year without seeing another woman. I treasured the moments of fellowship I had with Mary Burnett, after she became our neighbor. A day was set aside to go and visit Mrs. Burnett. However, a man borrowed our wagon. It now seemed that our visit must be put off for a long time, as it would be out of the question to leave home during the lambing season, which had just begun. But the yearning to see my friend was so strong that I decided to walk and carry the baby. I set out early in the morning, went slowly, and was not overly tired. I enjoyed the visit; I had the talk and was satisfied. On our return, the Burnett family accompanied us part of the way. I never afterwards had the longing to see a woman as strong upon me, but I always cherished the deep friendship I had with Mary Burnett. I seldom saw another woman during those early years on the ranch.

*   *   *

In 1861, Mary Kennedy gave birth to Thomas Burnett, the first child born of the marriage of Mary and Wesley Burnett. When Thomas was two years old, Mary took him to visit friends in Santa Clara. There he took sick with the "bloody flue" and died after a brief illness. The mail service during the time was poor. Wesley did not know of his son's death until he went to Santa Clara to bring Mary and his son home. Thomas was buried in the cemetery at Santa Clara.

In December, 1863, Mary gave birth to her first daughter, Rosamond Burnett, in their Nacimiento cabin. While she was still a baby in arms, Mary took Rosa, as she was called, and her two-year-old brother, J. K. (James Kennedy Burnett), on the 140-mile jolting and dusty stage coach journey to visit her parents, who were then living in Los Gatos. On their return home, Wesley met them at Pleyto with the wagon and his team of mules, for the twenty-five-mile trip back to the ranch. On their way, a soaking rain fell and the adobe road became extremely slippery. The mules were unshod. Getting firm footing as they pulled through the mud was very difficult.

At one place the wagon trail ran along the backbone of a ridge. The top of the ridge was narrow and on the side was a bluff that dropped a hundred feet into the rock canyon below. Mary was in the front seat with Rosa and J. K. was in back of the seat, by a heavy trunk. When they reached the point opposite the bluff, the mules lost their footing and slid toward the edge of the road. Mary threw Rosa from the wagon and then jumped out herself. Because he was jammed behind the trunk, J. K. could not get out of the wagon. On the edge of the bluff was a small oak tree. The wagon tongue struck the center of the tree, and with that, the wagon and team came to a sudden stop.

Wesley unhitched the mules and somehow, with ropes tied to the wagon, got the mules to pull the wagon back on the road. Mary and the children walked down over the slippery ridge to a place where it was safe to get back in the wagon for the rest of the trip home. How a tragedy was averted became a family story for many years to come.

In 1864, near the end of the Civil War, a tremendous drought hit California, which eventually forced the Burnett family off their Nacimiento homestead. For lack of feed, nine hundred of their herd of a thousand cattle died. Thus, in the fall of 1865, the family moved to the coastal area of San Luis Obispo County, where there was more feed.

Because of the close relationship between the Kennedy and Lynch families, Mary and Wesley gave their homestead ranch on the Nacimiento to James and Alice Lynch. It is important for the following generations to note the dominant Christian character traits of compassion, love, hospitality and generosity demonstrated by Mary and Wesley throughout their lives. How they successfully balanced these gifts with their indomitable pursuit of position, wealth and worldly success, even during times of great loss and tragedy, remains an inspiration for all who follow.

Mary, Wesley and their four children, John Cooper, Charles Cooper, James Kennedy (J.K. or "Bud") Burnett, and Rosa Burnett, took their wagons and stock over the Santa Lucia Mountain to establish their new home on Villa Creek. This was all supposed to be government land.

Not long after, two Spaniards, Pedro Marques and Santiago Hernandez, claimed the land was theirs under a previous land grant. The Burnetts then paid them six hundred dollars for a quit claim deed. It is too complicated to go into all of the details of the transaction, other than to say that in the end, a third party ended up with the Villa Creek property and the Burnetts lost out. Not only did they have to deal with this problem, but a couple more disasters hit.

First, massive rains, after the long California drought, hit the land. During the heavy rain and flood conditions, Villa Creek became jammed with driftwood above the house. This caused the water to overflow the creek and flood their home. In order to lessen the danger, Wesley dug a hole under the foundation log on the upper side of the house, where the water was backed up. Then he dug another hole on the opposite side of the house. This let the stream pass through, between the fireplace and the beds. For a night and a day this stream of water flooded through the house. Mary tied a horse next to the door all night to help the family escape, in case it became necessary. Their hogs and chickens were swept away to the sea. The Burnetts were left with ruined land, a battered house, and depleted assets.

After all of this, Mary suffered an injury, which eventually contributed to her early death. This is how it happened. Mary's brother, Robert Kennedy returned from the Civil War and came to see her and her new family. One Sunday Robert Kennedy saddled a mare, Nancy by name, and mounted her with the intention of calling on a neighbor. The horse refused to go ahead. Instead Nancy reared backward. Mary felt it necessary to strike the horse on the rump, so her brother could   gain control. With that, the mare kicked Mary, injuring her right side. From that time on, Mary "suffered a weakened constitution," her son J. K. reported. In spite of the lingering injury, Mary bore three more children, Helen, Lillie and William, before she died thirteen years later in 1878.

The family always believed that the kick from the horse was partly responsible for Mary's early death.

*   *   *

While being evicted from the Villa Creek property, in May 1865, a new friend, Juan Jose Castro, proposed to sell his adjoining ranch to Wesley and Mary Kennedy. The ranch consisted of about three thousand acres, a large part of the historic Geronimo Grant. The land stretched a quarter of a mile northwest of present day Cayucos and up along the coast for two and a half miles. (As this history is being written in 2007, the pristine property between Highway One and the sea remains the same as it did in 1865, protected by governmental mandate.) Wesley told Castro that it would be impossible for him to buy such a large place, in view of the fact that he had little money and very little stock. "I will sell it to you on credit," Castro said. He was determined that the Kennedys should buy his land. This is mentioned because Mary, in many respects, appears to have had great influence on Wesley, a man of unusual strength, faith and independence.

Their son, J.K. Burnett, records, "My mother would pray for divine leadership in the transactions the family made. I heard her say many times, 'I am convinced God is giving us this Coast Ranch.' When this happened, my father consented to buy the famous Geronimo Grant."

The deed was signed on May 26, 1866. This proved to be the most fortunate transaction the Kennedy family ever made. Many of the events that happened, while the Kennedy family lived on the Coast Ranch near Cayucos, are recorded in the memoirs written by their son, J. K Burnett, and gleaned from the local papers of the time. From this wealth of material, incidents that applied to Mary Burnett and her two older sons, John and Charles Cooper, the step-sons of Wesley Burnett, came the following stories. They give added knowledge and insight into the life of Mary Kennedy Burnett, this remarkable pioneer mother.

*   *   *

After the devastating flood at the Villa Creek Ranch, the Kennedy family prepared to move their remaining stock down to the new Coast Ranch, Before they could make the move, a great fire swept the country. There was plenty of warning however, as clouds of smoke could be seen coming closer for days before it reached the new ranch. Because of the heavy spring rains, the country was covered with an enormous growth of dry grass, mostly wild oats. There

20

was an old dirt wagon road that ran through the ranch, parallel with the sea. As noted, this road later became part of California Scenic Highway One.

Before the actual move, Charles and John Cooper had driven all of the stock to the new ranch. Now they were faced with the challenge of saving all the Kennedy stock from the sweeping grass fires. Fortunately, there was a protected area between the Coast Road and the sea, to which they drove the stock, In this way, they saved all the animals, except for one hog that failed to get below the road. That hog stayed in the creek a half-a-mile above the road. Unfortunately, he did not have the sense to stay there. The hog jumped out of the creek and tried to outrun the fire. The fire overtook him and he was burned to a crisp. There was a north wind blowing, and at times the fire traveled as fast as a horse could run.

Wesley selected the building site for the new home. It was located a short distance up a little valley that ran down to the coast wagon road, a mile-and-a-quarter west of Cayucos. The road is still there today. There is a creek that runs down the valley, past the remains of the old Burnett home, under Coast Highway One, which was a wagon road then, and empties into the ocean lagoon. This Big Creek, as they called it, drained the heart of the ranch. Little Creek ran into Big Creek where the house is located.

The Burnett cabin was built of pine lumber bought at a sawmill near the present town of Cambria. As soon as the walls were up and the roof was on the main part of the house, the Kennedy family moved in. J. K. Burnett remembers the night they arrived after the wagon trip from Villa Creek to the new Coast Ranch:

It was after dark. We built a fire on the dirt floor in the center of the room. A bear skin was laid down near the fire. Mother sat down on the bear skin and held the baby, Helen. Rosa and I sat nearby. There was still dry grass on the floor. I commenced to burn this off, a small patch at a time, Rosa wanted to burn some of the grass, too, but Mother said, "No, Rosa, don't you set any fires. Let Bud burn the grass and you watch him. We don't want too many fires going at once." I got to go on with my burning. I remember it as the first important mission of my life. Mother, early in their lives, always gave responsibilities to her children.

While living on the coast, Mary, on occasion, would visit her parents who lived in San Jose. The fastest transportation was by stagecoach. The stage carried mail, passengers and Wells Fargo Express, which was often quite valuable. On one of these return trips, several men rode their horses out of the willows, as the stage crossed the Salinas River north of San Miguel.

21

The would-be bandits were armed but not masked. They had every intention of holding up the stage. Mary recognized two of the boys, Tom and Young Selby from a neighboring ranch near Cambria. A local newspaper later reported: "Imagine Tom's astonishment when a well-known neighbor and family friend, Mrs. Burnett, looked out and said, "How do you do, Tom. What brings you over here?" The boys exchanged greetings and retired from the attempted robbery.

The following day the robbers attacked another stage, relieved the passengers of all their valuables and seized the Express box. After the thieves divided the spoils, Tom and his brother rode back to Cambria. On the way, a suspicious neighbor saw them and wondered why they were traveling so fast on spent horses so early in the morning. Officers were tipped off. The boys were soon arrested. The rest of the gang was located in the old town of Natividad. All were arrested, brought to trail, found guilty, and sent to prison. In the local paper, Mary Burnett was credited for foiling the initial robbery attempt, and later for identifying the young bandits. The stolen jewelry and money were later found and restored to the rightful owners. This ended the robber gang's dreams of quick riches and easy money.

Mary and Wesley took great pride in the horses they raised. The band thrived on the new Coast Ranch. Among the mares kept for breeding purposes was a well-bred mare named "Snip." When she was a colt her foreleg was broken, leaving her with a crooked leg. From then on she could never keep up with the regular band of horses. Her colts, no matter what their age, always stayed with her. She and her colts were called "Snip's Band." There would be a colt, a yearling, a two-year-old, a three-year-old, and sometimes a four-year-old, unless the four-year-old had been sold, which was the usual selling age. No matter how many times the band of horses would race past where Snip was located, not a colt ever left her to take up with the big band. Wesley sold several of his young horses, one of which was a "Snip's colt," to his friend Adam Bland, a Methodist preacher who lived in San Jose.

About a month later, Mary took her children on a spring wagon journey to visit her parents in San Jose. This was an adventurous undertaking for the young family. The second day out, while traveling the old stage road, Mary saw a Snip's colt coming back to the Coast Ranch at a full trot, making eight to ten miles an hour. He recognized Mary and her team. As he came close he halted for a moment, nickered to the horses, and then continued on his way back to Snip's Band. He was a splendid piece of horse flesh, about four years old, apparently stopping only for water until he arrived back at the ranch in record time.

Mary was not only a beautiful and feminine lady, she was a courageous person. Her son, J. K., tells of a tense experience he remembers when they lived on the coast:

Mother noticed two Spanish horsemen meet in the road below the house. They stopped, talked a few moments, and then left the road and started toward the house. Mother expected trouble. She hastily brought the ax in from the nearby woodpile, and then called for me, Helen, and Rosa to come into the house. We were playing on the bank of Little Creek. I could tell by the tone of her voice, she meant business! We instantly obeyed. Then she shut and locked the door. Mother took her stand inside the door, ax in hand. Charlie Cooper, her fifteen year old son, and our half-brother, took his place beside her with a cocked rifle in hand. Soon the horsemen rode up, and one dismounted and started toward the door. Mother said to Charlie, "If he forces the door, shoot right into his body and be sure you hit him!"

Charles replied, "I will!"

The man came to the door and said in Spanish, "Open the door!" Mother told him to clear out! Then he tried to open the door, but found it locked. Again, he yelled in Spanish several more times, "Open the door!" He kept trying to turn the knob. Mother kept yelling at him to clear out. This went on for several minutes. Finally, the Spaniard went back to his horse, and the two men rode away. Both men were heavily armed. Friends or foes, we were all satisfied that they were no friends of ours. Mother was a very brave person.

Mary took the children down to the lagoon soon after they arrived at the new ranch. They saw a mallard duck with twelve little ducklings swimming in the lagoon. She told the children, "The soil north of the lagoon is rich. This is where we will plant our gardens. It is a special spot."

From there they could see two large rocks. They rose out of the ocean at high tide and could be reached at low tide. The nearer rock was flat and covered with mussels. They named it Mussel Rock. The other rock was pointed, more like a tent, and had great cracks crowded with Abalone. They called this Abalone Rock. Many a fine mess of abalone or mussels came from these rocks. J. K remembers, "I became the abalone fisherman, and also the cooker of the abalone soup or chowder. I learned that after hammering the abalone to a pulp, it would not do to boil it; rather bring it to a boil and stop."

The time Mary spent with her children, exploring the land and beaches of Cayucos, brings warm memories to her children. They tell of the Indian Rocks they discovered on a jutting point north of the lagoon that they named Diamond

Point. Near that bank of the ocean is a very large rock, in which the Indians had drilled holes about six inches across. With a rock pestle, the Indians had ground their food in these rock mortars. (With these meager directions, many years later, Joan and I located the place, pristine now, as it was over a hundred years ago.) It was here, even with the harshness of the pioneer life, Mary found a quality of peace for a short time with her growing family.

Trinidad Castro, a son of Juan Jose Castro who sold the ranch to the Kennedys, came from his home in San Jose for a visit. He asked Wesley to let him pick a horse out of the band as a gift, and he selected a beautiful sorrel horse. Wesley objected to the proposition. Then Trinidad Castro said, "Mr. Burnett, you got the ranch so cheap, surely you don't object to me taking one horse from your large band. One of my work horses just died, and I need another horse to make a span."

Wesley left it for Mary to decide. "Well, Trinidad, we had picked that horse for our own use and he is not for sale to anyone. But under the circumstances, we cannot refuse you. You can take the horse as a gift." Trinidad was a happy man as he led the horse off the ranch bound for his home in San Jose. The horse was worth about one-hundred and fifty dollars. This story gives insight into the trusting relationship of two strong and competent human beings. They had a tenderness and appreciation that superseded the vicissitudes of their strenuous life together.

In 1869 Mary was left alone for two months with their six children while Wesley and several workers drove a thousand of their hogs to San Francisco to be sold. The details of this amazing drive are related in the Wesley Burnett chapter. Needless to say, this time of separation again placed tremendous responsibility on this pioneer mother. Her seven-year-old son, J. K., remembers his father's return.

I was outside the house and noticed a man driving a four-horse team coming up to the house. There was an erect eight-foot pole on one side of the wagon, around which was lashed a canvas. It was a strange looking outfit to me, so I called to my mother that someone was coming up the road. Mother said, "Why, don't you know who that is? It's your father." And so it was. The presents were soon unpacked. Mother was given a cloak with great flowing sleeves, which was in style then. I was given a new pair of red top boots, the first ones I had ever owned. They were too large by at least an inch in length, but this made no difference. I wore them everywhere except to bed. Later on I wore them to school and how they did squeak. The louder they squeaked the better I liked it. Finally, they wore out at the toes. Father sewed up the worn boots with buckskin and this gave them a new lease of usefulness. A pair of red-top boots in those days was sufficient to render a boy of my age distinguished.

*　　　*　　　*

In 1870 Mary and Wesley, after careful consideration and prayer, decided to go into the sheep business. A band of two-thousand head was purchased from a man named Woodward who lived on Torro Creek. When the sheep were first brought to the ranch, coyotes were very bad. One night eighteen sheep were killed by coyotes. From then on the Burnetts kept herders with the sheep at night. Each herder had a dog, and a lantern was hung out at the camp.

From then on, the main business on the Burnett ranch was sheep. In 1870 a landing was established at Cayucos. Schooners called occasionally and took away the wool. The wool was packed in large sacks weighing two-hundred-and-fifty to three-hundred-and-fifty pounds. There was no wharf at Cayucos in the first years of the harbor. The schooners anchored out in deep water and ran a surf-line ashore. Over this line surf-boats were pulled from the wharf to the ships with their load of lumber, grain and wool. At the height of his expansion, in 1881, Wesley Burnett had 44,000 sheep on his 20,000 acres of land. This was better than driving hogs to San Francisco.

*　　　*　　　*

The exact time Wesley and Mary left the coast is not known, but we do know they returned to their 360 acres of land in Adelaida sometime in 1872. Why, we can only surmise. It was a tumultuous year for this intrepid couple. Three major challenges occurred in 1872. They included the birth of their last child, William Wesley Burnett; the deteriorating health of Mary; and the traumatic loss of their nineteen-year-old son, John Alexander Cooper.

Here is the story. During the years that the family lived on the Cayucos Coast Ranch, John watched the great sailing ships ply the California coast. As the timeless and restless sea pounded the rocks along the shore, he looked beyond. What mystery lay out there over the distant horizon? He became captivated. In 1871, when he was eighteen years old, John Cooper came to Mary. "Mother," he said, "I have always dreamed of sailing on one of those great schooners to see the world. Someday, I want to be the captain of my own ship."

Mary's heart sank. She knew her men and their drive for adventure on new frontiers. With a heavy heart, she let John go.

In 1871, John Cooper left San Francisco, bound for the South Seas on the whaler Florence. Months went by and Mary heard nothing. Then, in 1872, she received word that John Alexander Cooper was dead! The ship was reported to have landed for supplies in the Pleasant Islands. (These islands are not noted on the world atlas, but it is presumed that they are located in the vicinity of New Zealand.) The report continued, "A native secreted himself on the ship. After the ship was at sea, he came out and said he wanted to be a sailor. A few days thereafter this native became insane and killed three men on the ship, John Alexander being one of them."

At the time of his death, he was studying navigation and was to have been promoted to an officer on the Florence. John was well on his way to fulfilling his dream of becoming the captain of a ship, and now it was ended. This tragedy occurred in March 1872. The Burnett family was devastated.

Little has been recorded about the four years from the time the family moved from the Coast Ranch until Mary's death at the famous Corral de los Mulos Ranch in Adelaida. We do know that in these years, Mary declined in heath, both physically and emotionally. A niece of Wesley Burnett, also named Mary Burnett, came from an unhappy situation with a stepfather in Illinois, to nurse Mary in the waning months of her life. This wonderful young lady was a tremendous help to Wesley and Mary Burnett and their family, during a time of great need. Mary Kennedy Burnett died in the ranch home at the Corral de los Mulos on January 20, 1878.

The deep mutual Christian faith shared by Mary and Wesley produced a love of unusual dimension. This love sustained them through the challenges and tragedies of their strenuous life. There was mutual respect, trust and admiration as they moved through the ups and downs of the human adventure. They were an effective parental team for a talented family. They modeled a spiritual foundation: a rich heritage for those who followed.

Wesley Burnett, in his love and grief, buried Mary among the oaks on a ridge above their Adelaida ranch home. From the front porch of the house, he could look up to the final resting place of his beloved companion and wife. For Wesley, the spark was gone, but the rich memories lived on.

*   *   *

During the Spanish American War, Wesley Burnett Jr. wrote an article for the San Luis Obispo <u>Weekly Breeze</u>, telling of his experiences in the Philippines. In the article was a poignant reference to his home in Adelaida and his mother, Mary Kennedy Burnett. He wrote:

I have many happy recollections of the hills of old Adelaida. It was there I grew up strong and healthy. But there are sad memories, too. My dear mother lies in the little cemetery on the hill—a pretty place for me, shaded by mighty oaks and a view of the Santa Lucia Mountains to the west. Home is not the same without her.

W. W. Burnett, Lieutenant, U.S. Army
Battery A. Artille, Manila, 1898
Spanish American War

MARY KENNEDY BURNETT
1830 – 1878

Mother of the frontier ... buried among the oaks on a ridge above her ranch home. Her deep Christian faith sustained her through the challenges and tragedies of her strenuous life ... a model for those who follow.

GENEALOGY OF MARY KENNEDY BURNETT

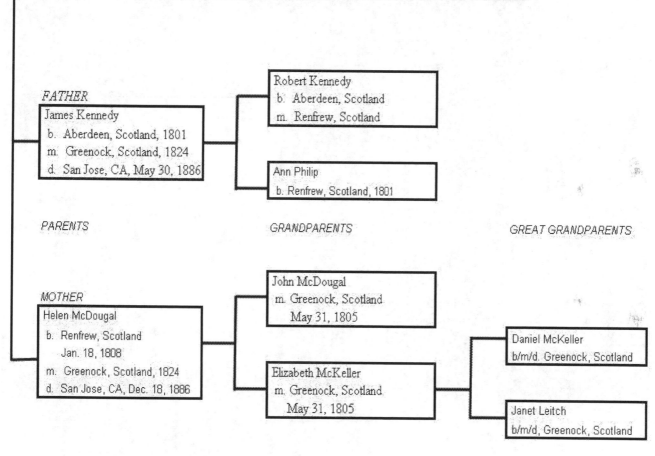

Mary Kennedy Burnett
b. 1830, Canada
m. Wesley Burnett, June 4, 1860
d. Jan. 20, 1878, Adelaida, CA

FATHER
James Kennedy
  b. Aberdeen, Scotland, 1801
  m. Greenock, Scotland, 1824
  d. San Jose, CA, May 30, 1886

Robert Kennedy
  b. Aberdeen, Scotland
  m. Renfrew, Scotland

Ann Philip
  b. Renfrew, Scotland, 1801

PARENTS   *GRANDPARENTS*   *GREAT GRANDPARENTS*

MOTHER
Helen McDougal
  b. Renfrew, Scotland
    Jan. 18, 1808
  m. Greenock, Scotland, 1824
  d. San Jose, CA, Dec. 18, 1886

John McDougal
  m. Greenock, Scotland
    May 31, 1805

Elizabeth McKeller
  m. Greenock, Scotland
    May 31, 1805

Daniel McKeller
  b/m/d. Greenock, Scotland

Janet Leitch
  b/m/d, Greenock, Scotland

MARY KENNEDY GRAVE
Adelaida Cemetery,
Paso Robles, California

The photo on the left is an untouched tombstone picture. The photo on the right has been enlarged and computer-enhanced by Don Dutcher to allow a closer view of the inscription. See the next page for a more detailed explanation.

```
┌─────────────────────────────────────────┐
│                                           │
│             MARY K BURNETT                │
│                                           │
│                  DIED                     │
│                                           │
│              JAN 10, 1878                 │
│                                           │
│                 AGED                      │
│                                           │
│               48 YEARS                    │
│                                           │
│                                           │
│                                           │
│      SEARCH THE SCRIPTURES; FOR IN        │
│                                           │
│     THEM YE THINK YE HAVE ETERNAL         │
│                                           │
│      LIFE: AND THEY ARE THEY WHICH        │
│                                           │
│      TESTIFY OF ME.  JOHN V: 39           │
│                                           │
└─────────────────────────────────────────┘
```

The scripture on the base of the Mary Kennedy Burnett tombstone (previous page) has been worn over the years, and is now difficult to read. But it is important to preserve this message of assured hope, so that all can read. Several translations of this passage of scripture were searched to determine the translation from which it had been taken, but to no avail.

Later, by chance, I discovered the well-worn personal Bible of my father, Franklin W. Robinson. I opened to the passage quoted on the Mary Kennedy monument. There, word for word, was the translation I sought. It was from a Bible published in Philadelphia by the John C. Winston Company and printed in Great Britain. There was only the following disclosure: "translated out of the original tongues, and with the former translations diligently compared and revised."

This Bible had been given to my father in 1911, on the occasion of his twenty-second birthday, by his mother, Rosamond Burnett Robinson, the eldest daughter of Mary Kennedy Burnett.

The New International Version of the Bible has been helpful in further understanding, John 5:39: *You diligently study the scriptures because you think that by them you possess eternal life. These are the scriptures that testify about me, yet you refuse to come to me to have life.*

F. Willard Robinson, 2005

THE SPRINGER FAMILY IN AMERICA

Sweden to England, 1676

England to Virginia, 1678

In Servitude, 1678 - 1683

Virginia to Delaware, 1683

Delaware to Kentucky, 1781

Kentucky to Indiana, 1806

INTRODUCTION TO THE
SPRINGER FAMILY IN AMERICA

In Volume I of <u>The History Of The Robinson Family</u>, the story of William Burnett and his wife, Mary Springer, were combined into a single chapter. This was because their grandson, J. K. Burnett, in writing the life story of his father, Wesley Burnett, reviewed the history of the Burnett family line. The Burnett lineage had been established back to the founding of Jamestown, Virginia in 1607. This story of the Burnett family history is covered in Volume I of <u>The History Of The Robinson Family</u>. Apparently, little was known of his grandmother Mary Springer Burnett's ancestral line.

Several years later, the excellent genealogical work of Louise and Sheldon Craddock became available. Louise Craddock is the great, great granddaughter of Mary Springer Burnett. The friendship and help of the Craddocks has now made it possible to reconstruct the amazing history of the Mary Springer Burnett family lineage. Here again, in some detail, is presented this important segment of family history. It is done with admiration and awe of the fortitude and steadfastness of these courageous ancestors.

FRANKLIN W. ROBINSON FAMILY
Relationship to Burnett and Springer Families

(marriage)

Christopher Springer ← **Beata Hendrickson**
b. Lamsbedt, Hanover, Germany 1593   b. Stockholm, Sweden
d. Stockholm, Sweden 1669   d. Stockholm, Sweden 1693

(descendants)
↓

Carl C. Springer ← **Maria Hendrickson**
b. Stockholm, Sweden 1658   b. Calson Hook, Pennsylvania 1664
d. Wilmington, Delaware 1738   d. Wilmington, Delaware 1727

Charles Springer (Jr.) ← **Margareta Robinson**
b. Wilmington, Delaware 1693   b. Wilmington, Delaware 1702
d. Wilmington, Delaware 1759   d. Wilmington, Delaware after 1768

Charles Springer (III) ← **Susanna Seeds**
b. Wilmington, Delaware 1728   b. Wilmington, Delaware 1730
d. Frederick Co., Maryland 1777   d. Fredrick Co., Maryland

John Springer ← **Sara Ann Butler**
b. Hagerstown Maryland 1756   b. (no record)
d. Washington Co., Kentucky 1816   d. Washington Co., Kentucky 1796

Mary Springer ← **William Burnett**
b. Frederick Co. Maryland 1780   b. Virginia 1776
d. New Lebanon, Indiana 1851   d. New Lebanon, Indiana 1863

Wesley Burnett ← **Mary Kennedy Cooper**
b. New Lebanon, Indiana 1818   b. Canada 1830
 (came to California 1850)   (to California via Indiana 1852)
d. Adelaida, California 1905   d. Adelaida, California 1878

Rosamond Robinson ← **John Wesley Robinson**
b. Nacimiento, California 1863   b. Monroe Co., Iowa 1855
d. Long Beach, California 1918   d. Berkeley, California 1936

Franklin W. Robinson ← **Hope Gould**
b. Grangeville, California 1889   b. Monterey, California 1893
d. Long Beach, California 1978   d. Long Beach, California 1958

CARL C. (CHARLES) SPRINGER
1658 - 1738

    Carl Christopher Springer, an illustrious ancestor, was the first of the Springer line to step foot in America. It was only when he became established in his new land that he anglicized his name to Carl. This has caused some confusion as the records are traced, but it has been well established that Charles C. and Carl Springer are one and the same. Thus, he shall be referred to as Carl C. Springer. Novelists have memorialized him in fiction and historians have searched the records closely for information about him. His notoriety is justified. This short history of Carl's eventful and productive life will help to establish the basis for the esteem in which he is held and confirm him as a model for future generations.

    The story of Carl Christopher Springer begins in Stockholm, Sweden where he was born in 1659, the son of Christoffer and Beata Salina Springer. His father was an official in the Swedish court, and in addition to his other duties as the archive inspector of the Royal Exchequer he also drew a salary as a musician. Christoffer had emigrated from Germany and became a naturalized citizen of Sweden, rising rapidly to a position in the King's court. He was widowed twice. Beata, Carl's mother, was Christoffer's third wife. These were difficult and yet rewarding years for this patriarch.

    Beata, Carl's mother, was the eldest daughter of Dr. Baltzar Salinas, the court physician to the King of Sweden. These connections gave the Springer children access to the ruling class, and with it opportunities for a good education, which were so important to this talented family. The Springers lived in a nice stone home that was located in the suburbs of Stockholm, opposite the east gate of the Santa Clara Lutheran Church, which the family attended.

The particulars of Carl's childhood are vague, but we do know that for his higher education he was sent to Riga, where he may have lived with his older half-sister, Christina. By the time he was eighteen, arrangements had been made for him to go to Johan Leyonberg, Sweden's Minister to England. To live for over a year in the impressive consulate, surrounded by servants and luxury, while continuing his education, would be a tremendous opportunity. So, on a summer morning in the year 1676, this boy of eighteen stepped from the doorway of his stone house, and turned to look at his mother's face for, what would prove to be, the last time. With his lips resolutely set, he entered the carriage that waited at the curb. A ship bound for England was being made ready to sail that day, and upon this vessel young Carl would board, never again to set foot on his Swedish homeland.

Carl spent a little over a year in London, learning his lessons well and completing his studies, particularly those in the English language. It neared the time to return home and his heart was full, because soon he expected to see his loving family again. It was not to be. While on a London street one night, he was set upon by ruffians. They bound him, and he was taken under duress aboard a merchant vessel in the Thames. He was kidnapped! The English ship immediately set sail across the Atlantic, bound for Virginia in the new world. Carl would be sold into servitude like an animal at market for a period of five years. To one of such sheltered life, a student by disposition and training, the five years that followed might well have been an almost intolerable experience, leaving deep scars of bitterness and hatred. Instead, Carl grew into a man full of stature.

When the term of his servitude was over, Carl Springer made his way northward to the Swedish settlement of Christina. He had heard about the people from his homeland that were on the Delaware River. The record of his long life of service in Wilmington occupies an important place in the early history of our country. How this all happened to him was told many years later in a letter he wrote to his mother.

June 1, 1693

My highly honored, dear Mother, I cannot allow this occasion pass which I now have, thank God, without making known to you, dear Mother, my doings and life at this time. First of all, it is deplorable to be so far away from my mother, brothers, relatives and other family connections, particularly as I cannot get any communications from you for all that I have written to you, except for one letter received in England. I am writing to you to let you know about my coming to this country. When I was in London and had in mind to return to Sweden,

38

my native land again. Here in England I had gone to school, learned the English language, reading, writing, and became well-versed in the art of arithmetic—as I say, when I was about to return home again, I was kidnapped and against my will taken on board an English ship, and also contrary to my will, was brought to America in the West Indies in Virginia. When I arrived there I was sold like a head of cattle being brought to market, and was thus sold at auction to work, and held in the worse slavery for altogether five years. My work was unbearable; it was extraordinarily severe in the summer in the daytime; in the wintertime my work was to clear land and to cut down the woods and to prepare the soil for the planting of tobacco and Indian corn. I have—to God be praise, honor, and glory—overcome it all.

When I had faithfully served my time, I heard accidentally that there were Swedes at the Delaware River in Pennsylvania, which formerly during the Swedish regime was called Nya Sverige. As I said, I undertook the burdensome journey of some four hundred miles, and when I arrived there I met the old people and they treat me in a very friendly manner. When I had been there about a year and a half, it pleased God to send and vouchsafe me a most virtuous wife by the name of Maria Hindrichsdotter, whom I married December 27, 1685, and with whom it pleased God to vouchsafe me three children, all three of my daughters; and she is even now with her fourth child. May God Almighty grant her a good delivery.

As regard to my activities here, I wish to say that I am a reader in the only Swedish congregation here and serve it because now we have no ministers in this country, for they are all dead. I serve the congregation and the church by reading the word of God and explaining to the congregation on the basis of a Swedish book of homilies and the singing of the hymns. Thus I have served the congregation going on the fourth year. And besides this, I have two plantations, which I have bought, and on them alone I live and move about, sowing all kinds of seed during the year. Also I have livestock for the needs of the people of my house, and I live, God be praised, in such a manner that I and mine suffer no wants.

My highly honored Mother, Dear, now let me hear from you and my dear brothers—if they are alive or not and how they are situated. God knows my sorrow for not have news from you. It would make me heartily glad, and it has been my highest desire before I depart this life, that I may hear of your good situation. We here in this land have lately experienced something extraordinary—we who are Swedes. We have received a letter in this land from our king in Sweden to the effect that he, upon hearing our communication and admonition, will send us ministers and Swedish books of which there is great need; for the people here have no one among themselves besides me to write for them, which I have done. And I ask you also, my dear beloved mother to please send me manuals and hymnals, because I have none besides my own. And will you please send it addressed to me along with some acquaintance to Gethenburg to the honorable, faithful servant, and postmaster, Johan Thellin, who, no doubt, will send it to me by the first ship sailing. I am very embarrassed here, dear Mother, because of the lack of books.

It has been my great sorrow in this land that I am so far from you. I cannot help but feel that way. I am sending herewith greetings to my dear brothers, and my dear brother Lorentz Springer, his wife and children. Greetings to all good friends and relatives and all who know me by name. My dear wife and my children send greetings, as well as others in the community—and while remaining your most obedient son even unto the death,
I am Karell Christoferrson Springer

The sequence to this letter is interesting. In addition to the three daughters referred to in the letter, Carl and Maria's family grew until they had seven sons and another daughter, making a total of eleven children.

It is doubtful that Carl's mother ever received his letter; at least he never received an answer from his mother. It has been suggested that if she had been living to receive it, this very personal letter would probably not have gone into the Royal archives. Research in Stockholm, however, quite definitely established her death as 1714, many years after the letter was written. But, by some strange sequence, his letter eventually was found in the Royal archives in Stockholm, a valued communication detailing life in the far off original Swedish settlement in Wilmington on the Delaware. The interesting contents of the letter and its arrival at a time when all Sweden was eager for more word from the New World, no doubt explain its preservation. The fact that she was a nurse to the Queen may also help to explain the presence of the letter in the Royal achives. This was particularly important because there had been a period of nearly forty years following the withdrawal of the Swedish colonial government in 1655 that there was virtually no communication between the settlements on the Delaware and the homeland.

Many letters had been written urging the sending of supplies, a minister, and all other things needed for the colony. They were sent on Dutch and English ships, but few, if any, ever reached Sweden. There were no replies. What tremendous excitement then prevailed when on May 23, 1693, a letter was received from John Thelin, Postmaster of Gothenburg, expressing the king's interest in the condition of the American settlers, and asking for news of them!

Carl Springer translated the letter for Deputy-Governor William Markham and was chosen to prepare the answer, on behalf of the entire Swedish community, "he being now the most suitable among them to write Swedish and to read Swedish writing". Fortunately, his letter reached Sweden safely and is preserved, along with the letter to his mother, in the Royal Archives in Stockholm. Its clear picturing of the life of the community at that period is invaluable.

As a result of his letter, the King in 1696 sent a missionary as well as many of the Bibles, Catechisms, and Prayer books they requested. It was a great day when the new missionary arrived. He was the Reverend Erick Bjorn. Reverend Bjorn found, to his surprise, that Carl Springer had, in the absence of a minister, been serving for four years as a lay reader at the Crane Hook Church. When the new Holy Trinity Church was built, Springer aided Pastor Bjork in obtaining the money to pay for the building of the church. Following the completion of the church in 1698, Carl was instrumental in enabling the church to acquire additional land. A large tract, occupying much of the present site of Wilmington, became available. These 500 acres were conveyed to Carl Springer, acting as the primary trustee of the church. In the conveyance of these many parcels by deed or long-term lease, Carl Springer continued to act as trustee and Warden for the church. It was undoubtedly a misconception that Carl ever owned these properties, for he only managed them for the church. Regardless, many years later a great number of individuals announced themselves to be Springer heirs to claim the large tracts of Wilmington real estate, which they contended he owned. They were never successful in their claims.

Aside from the positions of trust bestowed upon him by the congregation of Holy Trinity, known as the Old Swedes Church, he was also recognized by the civil authorities. In 1726 he was appointed a Justice of the Court of Common Pleas of New Castle County and the following year he was commissioned a Justice of the Court of Oyer and Terminer for the same county. The English language, reading and writing, which Charles knew so well, because of his rich education proved very helpful to him and his associates for the duration of his life. He continued to help his friends in Christina in business transactions with their English neighbors.

Maria, his faithful wife, died in 1727. Following her death, Carl married Annika Justis Walraven, daughter of John (the Elder) and Brita Justis, the widow of Jonas Walraven, Carl's long-time friend and fellow vestryman at the Holy Trinity Church where they had all been so active.

It is sad to realize that this wonderful ancestor never returned to his beloved homeland and the warm family he had left so many years before. It is apparent that he never knew what had happened to his parents. There is no mention of his father in the records as recounted by Carl. Records indicate that his father died shortly after Carl left Sweden. We do know that his father died in Stockholm, Sweden in 1669. He had accumulated adequate financial resources to provide well for his wife Beata Henrickson Springer, who apparently lived over fifty years as a widow.

Carl Springer, by all accounts, remained active for many years, not only with his church responsibilities, but also in his high judicial positions until his death, at the age of 80 years, on May 26, 1738. He was appropriately buried close to the church for which he labored so long and earnestly. Thus was lived out the life of this ancestor, a life that future generations can review with pride. He was a man who believed in honest toil, a worthy education, and a quiet upright living of service. He disliked pomp or show. It was perhaps these traits, coupled with energy and tenacity that enabled many of his descendents to make their mark, too, on the wild and challenging lands of the new frontier. Many did contribute mightily in the opening of the West. May members of the current generation live their lives with a quality that insures a similar legacy of integrity and spiritual contribution.

*   *   *

In the event that the name "Carl" Springer might be misleading as presented in this account, in the latter years of his life he assumed the name, Charles Christopher Springer, Sr. Therefore, Carl (1658-1738) and Charles Christopher, Sr. (1658-1738), are one and the same person.

Because Delaware's Old Swedes Church in Wilmington has been so much a part of the Springer family heritage, it is well that it is put in perspective. The church was built in 1698, largely under the leadership of Carl Springer. It is surrounded by 15,000 graves and is perhaps better known in Sweden than by most Americans. Each year individuals and groups from Sweden make emotional pilgrimages to the historic stone-and-brick edifice, which is the oldest Protestant church still standing, as originally built, in the United States. More important, in all these years it has never ceased to be regularly used for religious services.

The original colony established Old Swedes Church as a Lutheran congregation. In 1791, when the Swedish ministers stopped coming to the new work, Old Swedes became an Episcopal church, a denomination that has continued to this day.

Many of the church's possessions are gifts from the Swedish royal family and from towns and organizations in Sweden. These gifts include an alter cloth given to the church in 1950 by King Gustav Adolph V. who embroidered the central cross himself, a copy of a prayer book used in Sweden during the Colonial period. There is also a 1540 Swedish Bible, a gift from the Crown Prince of Sweden in 1938.

Old Swedes Church is a spotless sanctuary with room for 250 worshippers in its quaint white box pews. The original black walnut pulpit and canopy is said to be the oldest pulpit in use in America. A hand-carved black walnut dove suspended from the canopy is a gift from Sweden. The church floor is made of bricks fired and laid in 1698. It is a humbling thought to realize that those who lived out a spiritual commitment of this historic dimension, passed on in part, the genes we inherited.

HOLY TRINITY (OLD SWEDES) CHURCH

Holy Trinity is the oldest church in the United States that has held continuous services from 1699 until the present day. The dedication of Holy Trinity Church in 1669 was a milestone in the remarkable success story for one of its members, Charles (Carl) Christophersson Springer, who had come from Sweden some twenty-two years after the Dutch seizure of New Sweden. It was he who wrote the 1693 letter asking for new Swedish ministers on the Delaware. It was he who lent his tireless assistance to pastor Eric Bjork in the negotiations necessary to accomplish their goal of constructing the new church. And it was he who Bjork singled out as the most important reason for the success of this venture.

The following generations look to the Holy Trinity Church as a living monument, not only to our Lord, but to the tenacity, dedication and Christian commitment of their illustrious ancestor who began the Springer family line in America, Charles (Carl) Christophersson Springer.

CHARLES SPRINGER (JR.)
1693 - 1759

The story of Charles Springer will not be one of great adventure, like so many of our other ancestors whose restless spirits kept them moving with the new frontier. Charles Jr., (the "Jr." is used to distinguish between the three generations of Charleses in the Springer line, remained all of his life in what is now Wilmington Delaware. He was a substantial businessman and loyal husband to his wife, Margareta Robinson. This venerable couple raised twelve children. The records establish the following information about their lives.

Charles Springer (Jr.) was born at Oak Hill in Christiana Hundred, New Castle County, Delaware in 1693. He died at the same place sixty-six years later. He was buried August 26, 1759, at Holy Trinity Church. Charles married Margareta Robinson in 1722. His wife, Margareta Robinson was also born at Christiana Hundred, 1702. We know she was still living there in 1768, because she was named on the Holy Trinity Church list as one of those taking communion in the Swedish language.

Charles Springer (Jr.) and his wife Margareta Robinson had twelve children, all baptized at Holy Trinity Church. Charles (III), their fourth child, is the one who is in our direct ancestral line.

- Maria, born 25 June 1723, married Nils Justis {Swedish} 1742, died New Castle County, Delaware after 1774
- John, born 9 August 1725, married Mary Welsh, 20 November 1747, moved to Frederick County, Maryland, where he died after 1765.
- Anna, born 17 December 1727, married John Smith {Swedish} in 1744. He died by 1753. She appears to have remarried Andrew Vaneman {also Swedish}.

- <u>Charles (III)</u>, born 17 December 1728, married Susanna Seeds, \9 April 1752, moved to Frederick County, Maryland, where he died in 1777.
- Catharina, born 21 November 1731, married Thomas Ogle, Jr. 2 June 1750, died in Christiana Hundred and buried June 17 59.
- Edward, born 24 January 1734, moved to Virginia where he married Catherine Graham, and died in Fayette County, Kentucky
- Jacob, born 19 February 1737, married his cousin Catherine Springer 27 April 1763, died in Christiana Hundred. 1773.
- Gabriel, born 10 May 1739, married Elizabeth Tranberg {widow of Rev. Olof Parlin of Gloria Dei Church, Philadelphia} 14 January 1762, died 12 August 1781 in Wilmington. He died childless and his will left 10 Pds. To each of his brothers. In addition, he gave to Charles Springer (son of his brother Charles, and our direct ancestor) " my present dwelling and hatter's shop on the west side of Market Street between 2nd and High, plus the pasture being rented from Peter Stalcop fronting on High and 2nd. Streets (New Castle County wills,
  L: 250-252.)
- Margareta, born 27 May 1741, married her cousin Charles Josephsson Springer on 28 October 1759, and was buried 23 August 1820 in New Castle County.
- Rachel, born 6 June 1743, died in childhood.
- Rebecca, born 2 July 1746, married John Armstrong 10 May 1764 and died before 1804 in Christiana Hundred.
- Elizabeth, born 18 February 1747, married Samuel Walker about 1765 and died in 1823 in Allegheny County, Pennsylvania.

This is neither a colorful nor a delineated history for this important ancestor. But the life record of Charles Springer does denote stability, a loyalty and a dedication that were so much a part of the American dream. Along with adventure and daring, may we also be tempered with those qualities given us by Charles Springer (Jr.). His life was rooted in stability, service, loyalty, and faithfulness to his God.

CHARLES SPRINGER (III)
1728 - 1777

    Charles Springer, the son of Charles Springer (Jr.) and Margaretta Robinson, was born on December 17, 1728, at Oak Hill in Christiana Hundred, New Castle County, Delaware. He spent his youth there in the Wilmington area with the Swedish families, whose lives centered around the Old Swedes Church where his late, departed grandfather had been such a pillar.

    As he grew into manhood, he fell in love with a beautiful young lady he had known all of his life. Susannah Seeds, two years younger than Charles, had also been born in Christiana Hundred, New Castle County. This is all now a part of the Wilmington area of Delaware. Charles and Susannah were married in the Holy Trinity (Old Swedes) Church in Wilmington, Delaware, on April 7, 1752. The large families were all there to celebrate the union.

    It is apparent that some of the young people were restless and wanted to strike out on their own. Maryland's liberality made the province an asylum for non-conformists. The development of the colony took on a cavalier spirit that appealed to many. Grants of land were being made directly to individuals. This promoted a diffuse population, which created a need and an impetus for the organization of territorial units for the purposes of local government. Nothing like this was possible in the northern colonies. Charles and his bother John, along with their new brides, Susanna and Elizabeth, who were the daughters of John and Brita Seeds, took off to make their homes in Frederick County, Maryland.

    It didn't take too long for Charles to make his presence felt. Two years after the family's arrival in Frederick County, records indicate that in November 1754, he served on the grand jury. A year later he was appointed as the "overseer" of roads from Major Ogle's Ford to John Brigg's Ford on the Monocacy River.

Charles Springer found himself a part of history in 1757, when he served as a sergeant in the French and Indian Wars. It is helpful to put his experience in context. The French and Indian Wars lasted from 1689 until 1763. During this time there was a continuing struggle between the French and the English for the entire drainage area of the Mississippi and Ohio River Valleys. English land speculators, as well as fur traders, had become active west of the Appalachian Mountains. They sought the control of the choice locations in anticipation of the coming settlers. The encroachments by the British in the area caused an alarm to the French, who had a claim on the area. The Indians had become friendly with the British, with whom they had traded. The war had intensified in 1753, as the opposing forces of England and France engaged in a final race for the possession of the Ohio River Valley. At the time the colonies were siding with the British, because they were a part of England.

The French, to counter the moves of their enemy, established forts on the Ohio River, the key to which was Fort Duquesne at the forks of the Ohio River. This is the present day location of Pittsburgh. Meeting the French challenge, the Virginia government sent George Washington a second time with a force to drive out the intruders. He was only partially successful because of the differences he had with the British in how to conduct the war. The falling out between him and the British commanders came because the English knew nothing about the techniques of frontier warfare. The Indians always presented a moving target, and of course, always wanted to side with the winners. So, as the French began to gain more control throughout the Ohio River Valley, the Indian loyalty shifted to the French.

The years 1756 and 1757 brought fresh disasters for the British. They had been compelled to surrender many of their previous advances. Swarming bands of French and Indians spread terror and desolation throughout the frontier. Cherokees, who had previously joined the British, because of their promise of lands and protection, now became troublesome and left the campaign. On their way back to their Indian enclaves, it was widely believed by the settlers that they had been the ones that had killed cattle, stolen the horses, and destroyed many of the farms on the frontier. In their suffering, the colonists took up arms, forming state militias.

Charles, who was twenty-nine years old at the time, and a sergeant in the militia, joined in the counter attack against the Indians. His little son, John Springer, was less than a year old at the time.

The foray on the frontier was short-lived. But, in the skirmishes, which ensued, a number of Cherokees were killed. The Indians were awed at the numbers of militia involved against them and soon retreated. The militias restored peace on the colonial frontier.

Following Charles' return from this adventure, he and Susanna were together for twenty more years. They raised a family of ten children, residing at their home on Lot #37 in Monocacy Manor as depicted in Tracy & Dern, Pioneers of Old Monocacy. Their beautiful 113-acre estate was later known as *Bell's Delight*. Following John's death in 1787, Mrs. Singer continued to live in the family home for at least ten years. On October 3, 1778, Susannah Springer, widow of Charles Springer, filed her accounts as administratrix of the estate. She reported a total inventory of 415 pounds (£), of which 391 remained after payment of debts. This was a most comfortable estate that was passed on to her children. Susanna on March 7, 1789 married John Silver, and so far as we can determine lived out her life with him. Thus ends the story of this venerable generation that carried on the history of our family during the time our nation was born.

JOHN SPRINGER
1756 – 1816

John Springer, the father of Mary Springer Burnett, was born in or near Hagerstown, Maryland about 1756. He was the second son of Charles Springer Jr. and Sara Ann Butler Springer, and his boyhood home was in or near Frederick City, Maryland. Frederick is located some fifty miles west of Baltimore. John grew up as an active boy during a time when there were several political forces emerging. One became the issue of who owned the frontier lands beyond the coastal settlements of the colonies. Another was the desire of the colonies to come together in some kind of confederate form of government, which would give them added strength against the imperial power of England. Within all of this uncertainty, the workers began to band together with the independent spirit of the frontier settlers for their rights against the power of the landed wealthy. Amidst all of this turmoil were the economic and political issues that were developing between the colonies and England. Not only was it a matter of unfair taxation and domination, but it was also the issue of who was to control the new lands west of the Appalachian Mountains. At that time England was siding with the Indians to block colonial expansion.

Young John sensed that one day he would be embroiled in these emerging conflicts. It was an accurate omen, for he was destined to play a part in this conflict. Thus, when he was twenty years old, he served in the Revolutionary War, entering the Maryland Militia from Frederick County, Maryland, under the command of Valentine Creager. This was October 3, 1776.

John Springer served only for a short time, before he was asked to join a Daniel Boone expedition. This force was to open a trail over the mountains to the Kentucky frontier. In one sense, the colonies were fighting a two-front war, one against the British along the coastal regions, and the other on the frontier

51

against the Indians, who were supported by the British. Boone took thirty riflemen and axe men to cut the Wilderness Road to Kentucky. They needed a supply route to hold off the Indians and the British. Also, the Colonists knew the only way to successfully claim the rich Kentucky land was to flood the area with settlers. It was imperative they develop a new route over the mountains, because they were much too vulnerable to ambush when floating down the old river routes. The brave men that John joined were what we would call today, fighting military engineers. The cutting of the Wilderness Road made a great contribution to the success of the colonies in the Revolutionary War. The road traversed a wilderness of trees, brush, mountain laurel, and rhododendron. It crossed creeks and rivers, and surmounted the mountains. This gateway to the West was the first route across the Appalachian Mountains to Kentucky. At first it was wide enough only for pack animals. Later the trail was widened for wagons. Thus it truly became the gateway to the West, as hearty pioneers crossed the Appalachian Mountains, and developed farms on the rich Kentucky lands. They would be the ones that would save the Northwest, keeping the Indians under control, and the British from having a free hand in the West, during the Revolutionary War.

John Springer later told his son about the hardships of the winter expedition.

I was sent out hunting to try to get some meat, because we were running so low on food," he said. "I walked and walked without a sign, then I saw a wild turkey gobbler that was starving to death. The snow was so deep he couldn't find any food. I scraped away the snow and placed the poor bird in the little cleared place. I had a handful of parched corn that I carried in my shot bag for nourishment, so I divided what I had with the turkey and left him to eat it.

Many years later this story continued to be told—how this act of kindness to the poor turkey was evidence that John Springer had a big, kind, and loving heart.

*   *   *

The Daniel Boone expedition was under the command of George Rogers Clark, and on the payroll of Thomas Moore's Company. The record of John Springer attests to the fact that he was paid, in November 1782: one pound for service on an expedition against the Indians. This was not too much for the agony, hard work and danger that he had endured, but it had opened his eyes to the rich Kentucky land. Soon this hearty and brave young family moved west

52

to take up land on the new frontier, first settling at Herrods Fort. This was necessary because the Indians were still troublesome. The woman stayed in the protection of the Fort, molding lead bullets, while the men stood guard and shot the attacking Indians. John's wife, Sara Ann Butler Springer and her sister Nancy Springer Silvers were leaders in this bullet-molding endeavor. The Springer family was fighting for their foothold on this new land, a fight that carried with it great peril. Fortunately, they had the protection of Harrods Fort to resist the attacks.

Others were not so fortunate. In 1782, George Rogers Clark was at the falls of the Ohio River. Because communication was poor, he was not aware of the determined attack being made by the Indians, again instigated and led by the British, against the frontier settlements. In this battle the Kentucky militiamen were put to rout with the loss of many men, and several of their commanding officers. None of the survivors of the massacre wanted to accept the blame for the blunder that had been committed. Someone finally suggested that the fault lay in the fact that Clark had failed to build certain forts, which he had been ordered to construct by the Governor. This was a futile and far-fetched excuse, but served to pass the buck. General Clark had tried to build the forts, but he had been supplied with neither the funds nor the men to help the beleaguered settlers.

When the problems with the Indians finally subsided, the Springer family moved near Springfield, Kentucky, and took up 160 acres of land that they developed into their home. There they would live for the rest of their lives. During this time, there was a tide of emigration to Kentucky. In 1784 land office fees were five times the total of the previous year. The infection of expansion had become a hectic fever. The rich land was coming into its own in a generous yield of crops. Log schoolhouses and churches were being raised among the clusters of cabins. Men, like John Springer, who had given their youth to the Revolution and to the opening of Kentucky, now gave their energies afresh to establishing their new homes.

John primarily farmed to sustain the family, but craftsmen were needed and he did have a set of tools, which he used from time to time to supplement the family needs. John and Sara Ann had eleven children. Mary our direct ancestor was the second child and their oldest daughter.

There was great sadness and despair in the family, when in 1797 John's wife Sara Ann died. Mary, who was only sixteen years old at the time assumed the major responsibility of caring for the children. She was a tremendous resource to her father, who toiled endless hours to provide for the family.

As happened so often in the lives of these brave frontier families, young children were left without a family or a father. It was a natural thing to have these families come together out of necessity. Often in these tragic situations, a love did develop, which gave great support in time of need.

This is what happened to John Springer, when about seven years later he married Elizabeth MacDonald, the widow of Samuel Ingram, and the mother of eleven children. The uniting of these two families now formed a family unit of twenty-two children. John and his new wife Elizabeth later had two children of their own. Apparently, this worked out well, because Mary Springer Burnett, the oldest daughter of John, later reported a great love and respect for her stepmother. As a matter of fact, there was such a wonderful relationship that after John Springer's death, Elizabeth made the trip to Indiana to live out her life with Mary, her stepdaughter. This expanded family kept close ties throughout the years. It is interesting to note a letter written to Ann Springer Ingram by her father John Springer.

Washington County, Kentucky, March 11, 1816

Dear Daughter,

I embrace this opportunity to let you know that we are all well at present, thanks be to God for his mercies, hoping these lines will find you the same.

I received your letter the 2nd. It gives us satisfaction to hear that you got safe through the inclemency of the weather. The evening you started, Betsey and myself were taken with the flue. I was not able to do anything for better than a month. Your mother (step-mother) was taken about the time of our Quarterly Meeting and kept her bed better than two weeks and she is very weakly yet. The rest of the children all had bad colds. Sally Peters has a son, and is well the last time I heard from them. She calls him John Springer Peters. John and the children are well. The rest of your brothers and sisters, friends and relations are well, but your Aunt Polly Silvers is dead and buried.

It is through difficulty I am yet striving for the hope of the Gospel. O, pray for us Anne. O, Anne do you strive for that one thing that is needful. Never rest till you know by blessed experience that religion will make you happy in time and in eternity.

We desire to be remembered to your father and mother to John Ingram and Rebecca. Peggy is much pleased with her beads and gives her kind love to you for them. Billy Ingram has started down the river. So no more at present, but I remain your loving father till death, John Springer

Peggy, of whom he speaks in this letter, is his daughter Margaret by his second wife. And Anne, to whom the letter is addressed, was her half-sister.

The latter days of John Springer's life not only dealt with the care and maintenance of his property, but court records mention that he continued his life long interest in road development. Between 1793 and 1800, it is noted that he served on a road committee to see what would be the best way to run a road from the Richard File place to the Mercer County Line. He also continued to be involved in the activities of the community Methodist Church.

John Springer, Revolutionary War participant, frontiersman, Kentucky settler and devoted father, died at his homeplace in Washington County, Kentucky in 1816.

MARY SPRINGER, 1780 – 1851
and
WILLIAM BURNETT, 1776 – 1863

Mary Springer was the epitome of the western pioneer woman. She knew little, from birth until death, but the frontal wave of the new America, as the hearty pioneers relentlessly moved west to establish their new lands, their homes and their culture. The first twenty years of her life, from childhood until her marriage to William Burnett, are related in the following sections of this chapter.

*   *   *

Mary, known as "Polly" for most of her life, was born on the Kentucky frontier in Washington County on May 9, 1780. (There has been some question about these facts in the family record. However, the record of Mary's birth is recorded in the *Washington County Marriage Records*, Book 1, page 43, as listed above. So we have some assurance that this information is accurate.)

Mary was the second of eleven children born of John Springer and Sara Ann Butler Springer. Mary's father had first made the trip to Kentucky late during the time of the Revolutionary War as a member of the Daniel Boone expedition. Boone was sent to help bring the Indians, who were supported by the British, under control. Although the frontier was a treacherous place at the time, the beauty and the fertility of the Kentucky land was impressive. So, upon return from this expeditionary experience, John Springer brought his new wife to the Kentucky frontier. They settled in Washington County, which is located some forty-five miles southeast of present day Louisville.

However, the tragic conflict with the Indians was far from over, and these early settlers were in continual peril. It was a time of disaster for all who fought for control of this beautiful land. Roving bands of Indians were everywhere, killing and scalping isolated settlers and burning their cabins. Two years after Mary was born, November 1782, negotiations were opened between the British and the colonies. General Washington was notified in a dispatch, "American independence is assured; the war is won!"

The treaty ending the Revolutionary War was signed in 1783. This ended the British support of the Indians in Kentucky, and although there were continued skirmishes, a rush of new settlers came to establish homes on the frontier. It was not until Mary was twelve years old that Kentucky became the 15th state in the Union.

When Mary was sixteen years old, her mother Sara died. This tragedy left ten younger children without a mother. Mary took over this responsibility and cared for all of her brothers and sisters. These years were especially hard for this pioneer family. But, Mary never shirked her responsibility and did a wonderful job in caring for the needs of the family.

When Mary was twenty years old she met William Burnett, a twenty-four-year-old young man from nearby Fayette County. William had come as a young boy to Kentucky with his mother from the Ohio frontier. He, too, had experienced a family tragedy. The following segment is the William Burnett story, up until the time he met and married Mary Springer. The history begins with Burnett ancestral roots in England and then America.

*   *   *

William Burnett's ancestors were early settlers in Virginia, having come to Jamestown from England during the settlement of the colony. The Jamestown records show there was a "Jo Burnett, age 24," who embarked from the ship *Abraham* of London in 1635. This well could be the first Burnett in America, for we know the family first settled in Virginia during the settlement of the original colony. The Burnetts traced their ancestry back to a Bishop Thomas Burnett, who was the Bishop of Canterbury in England. Over a century passed. Then, prior to the Revolutionary War, the Virginians, which included the Burnett family, were anxious to establish a claim on the Ohio River Valley. William Burnett's father, whose name we do not know, took his wife and three children into this wilderness with the first Virginia contingent of settlers shortly after the Revolutionary War began. Thus they became the original settlers of what would later become the State of Ohio.

As the Revolutionary War progressed, the Indians, encouraged by the British, began attacking the settlers. For mutual protection the men, armed with their single-shot rifles, formed squads and worked together to till their fields. While the men were at work, the woman and the children stayed together in a fort built for their protection.

One day William's father, in the company of about ten men, went to work a field for the planting of corn. On the border of the field there was a long log cabin where the men could go in inclement weather. There was a door at one end of the cabin and a fireplace at the other end. During this particular day a violent rain fell, so the men went into the cabin for shelter. As they entered, they stacked their rifles inside the door and went to the other end of the cabin to huddle around the fireplace. They had seen no signs of Indians during the morning and were not aware that a war party had been watching them from the woods. Now the Indians crept up, catching the men off their guard.

One of the Indians peered through a crack between the logs. Seeing the situation, he signaled to the rest. The Indians rushed in with their cocked rifles and cut off the men from their guns. The entire company was trapped. They had no choice but surrender. Thus, William's father was marched off with the others to the hostile Indian settlements.

After a few days travel, the war party divided, taking the men to different villages. The Indians immediately killed and scalped the men in one group. The others were taken to another Indian village as prisoners. William Burnett's father had been killed in the massacre. The Burnett family did not learn of the tragedy until some time later when members of the surviving party escaped their captors and returned to the terrified families, who had waited for weeks at the fort on the Ohio River for word. The young William lived with the image of the savage killing, as witnessed and described by the friends of his father.

Soon after, as usually happened out of necessity on the frontier, his mother remarried and took William and the other two children to Kentucky. This is where William grew into manhood. This is known because William Burnett's name is on the first census ever taken in Kentucky, in 1790. He lived in Fayette County and is listed on the March 19, 1790 tax rolls. It was during this time he met and fell in love with the beautiful and responsible lady of the frontier, Mary Springer. William and Mary were married in Kentucky, 1800. The historic story of William and Mary's life together now begins.

*   *   *

The year, 1800, was a bittersweet time in the history of the Burnett and Springer families. Mary had done an excellent job as a proxy mother. This is attested to by the fact that at the wedding Mary's father, John Springer, said to the bridegroom, "You are taking a piece of my heart." But life does have a way of going on. John Springer had eleven children by his first wife, Sara Ann Butler. Later he married Elizabeth Ingram, a widow with eleven children, and Elizabeth and John had two children. So between them, they had twenty-four children.

It is true, the attraction of the western frontier, even with all the hardship and tragedy involved, was still a tremendous pull on William and his new bride. So, after they were married, Mary and William decided they must cut a trail through to the Indiana Territory and strike out for themselves. This was a momentous decision for this brave and adventurous couple. They had to make their way through a trackless wilderness, for they were the first pioneers in this area of the Territory of Indiana to take up their own land. They had blazed the trail through the forests to mark the path of their journey. Long after, it was still known as the Burnett Blaze. It served for many years as the marked trail for the future settlers who came west to join the new settlement.

Shortly after their arrival the Indians went on the warpath against the settlers. This made life very uncertain. In self-defense the men oranized companies of rangers to quell the Indian attacks. The men, well mounted on their horses and equipped with long Kentucky rifles, took out after the marauding Indians. This left Mary alone at times to take care of the family responsibilities, and although difficult, she managed with courage and tenacity. What a relief if was for all, when William returned from these Indian campaigns to find his family still healthy and safe.

The Burnetts were not untouched by the War of 1812, for the settlers believed that England was behind the Indian resistance to their efforts to obtain land cessions. The Greenville treaty line had not long satisfied the land-hungry pioneers. The line established left almost the whole of Indiana within the Indian country, and William Henry Harrison, as the new governor of the Indiana Territory, was zealous in assuring these tracts for the settlers. The problem was that the new United States government was very ineffective at this time in resisting the British encroachments along the northern border. This was due to a lack of money, poorly trained officers, slow communication, and no roads over which to move troops and supplies. Thus it was a perilous time for the Indiana pioneers, who were essentially abandoned and left to their own resources. The War of 1812 was one of the most futile of conflicts, judged by the contrast between its objectives and the actual terms of the peace. The easy confidence with which the leaders had predicted a peace dictated at the

Canadian capital, contrasted sadly with the meager successes along the northern border. It took an enduring tenacity on the part of the pioneers to hang on to their gains—but they did persevere.

At 2:30 AM on Monday, December 16, 1811, the earth heaved and shook. The Burnett family lived at the epicenter of an historic earthquake, which occurred where no tremor had ever been recorded. There has never been a satisfactory scientific explanation for such a violent wrenching of the earth, and certainly it was a shock that left the people in a complete state of dismay. Worse, the initial earthquake was only the starter. The shaking continued intermittently for two terror-filled days. Cattle bellowed and kicked, lost their footing and were thrown to the ground. The settlers were tossed from their beds, heard the timbers wrench apart and watched the bricks crumble into heaps of debris. At the end of that time the atmosphere was so choked with dust and smoke that for a week afterwards the sun shone sickly reddish-bronze through an ugly haze.

Many of the neighbors became frightened. They came to the Burnett house for advice and help, fearing the end of the world was at hand. Mary reports that her husband William encouraged them to have faith in God and look to Him for help and protection. After William talked for a while, the settlers became reassured and returned to put their homes in order. The Burnett family was looked to for stability and leadership.

As the area in which Mary and William Burnett settled continued to grow, it became designated as the Gill Township in which the village of New Lebanon, Indiana, is located. Members of the family were devout Methodists, an evangelistic denomination that at that time had great appeal on the frontier of America. William and Mary were instrumental in establishing a Methodist Campground, where the summer revival meetings were held, and campers lived in bark tents. That location today is Mt. Zion Cemetery, the resting place of many pioneers of that era. The first meeting of a congregation of Methodists in this region was conducted by Reverend Shrader at the home of William and Mary Burnett in 1813.

This first meeting was an amazing thing, made possible by William having ridden his horse all the way back to Kentucky to locate a preacher who would come to Indiana. Ten years later they would build a frame meeting house, which they named the Mt. Zion Methodist Church. Then in 1830, at a cost of $1,000, the frame building was replaced with a brick church.

In the log cabin built on their wilderness farm, Mary and William raised ten children: eight boys and two girls. They were Joseph, John, James, Boone, Moses, Thomas, Wesley (our direct ancestor who was born on January 4, 1812), Cynthia and Susan. Practically the entire living of the family was produced on the farm. They had a few sheep and raised some flax, and with the wool and linen Mary (Springer) Burnett made clothing for the family. There was a sawmill on the farm, a gristmill, and a tannery. The Burnett farm was a busy and productive place. Oxen, working a treadmill, supplied the power.

Mary's father, John Springer, died in Kentucky in 1818. His second wife, Elizabeth, was left with two small children. Mary had been close to her stepmother. They had gotten along well, so it was natural that after the death of her father, Elizabeth made the difficult journey from Kentucky to Indiana to live with Mary in New Lebanon. Mary was always known for her generous and loving spirit.

In time, Mary saw her children grow up and leave home. One traumatic incident for the family occurred when her son Wesley, who was our direct ancestor, had taken a load of lumber and produce down the Ohio River to New Orleans. On this particular trip a serious cholera epidemic had hit the river. A neighbor from the Indiana settlement saw a man dying of cholera in a lumberyard in New Orleans that he mistook for Wesley. He positively identified the man he had seen dying as Wesley. Mary Burnett went into deep mourning. Then one day Wesley returned, walking through the front gate alive and well. His sudden and unexpected appearance was a great shock to Mary. But she soon recovered and there was great happiness and rejoicing in the family over the safe return of her son.

But Wesley did not stay home long, for soon news reached Indiana that gold had been discovered in California. The lure was too great. In the spring of 1850 Wesley left, leading a wagon train to the gold fields. Mary said good-bye to Wesley and watched him drive off in his wagons, never to see him again.

It was like a spark had gone out of the mother's life. Mary Springer Burnett died on December 14, 1851. This courageous and loving mother of the frontier gave much so that future generations would have the miracle of life and the chance to experience, each, their own unique journey. May the future generations remember this loving mother of us all with gratitude and admiration.

Twelve years later William, at the age of 84 years and eleven days, died on December 12, 1863. His life had spanned from the Declaration of Independence to the national turmoil and tragedy of the Civil War. He and his family had opened a frontier and, in his own way, had given leadership to the establishment of a young nation.

William and Mary Burnett are buried in the Burnett Cemetery, a short distance west of New Lebanon, Indiana.

SPRINGER ANCESTRY

Mary Springer Burnett married William Burnett in 1800. Children from their marriage included: Joseph, John, James, Boone, Moses, Wesley (our direct ancestor), Cynthia and Susan.

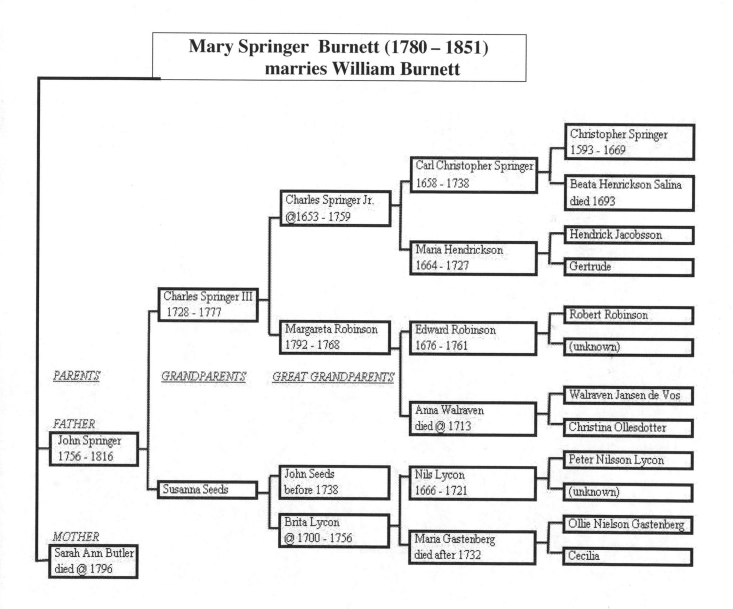

Mary Springer Burnett (1780 – 1851)
marries William Burnett

PARENTS *GRANDPARENTS* *GREAT GRANDPARENTS*

FATHER
John Springer
1756 - 1816

MOTHER
Sarah Ann Butler
died @ 1796

Charles Springer III
1728 - 1777

Susanna Seeds

Charles Springer Jr.
@1653 - 1759

Margareta Robinson
1792 - 1768

John Seeds
before 1738

Brita Lycon
@ 1700 - 1756

Carl Christopher Springer
1658 - 1738

Maria Hendrickson
1664 - 1727

Edward Robinson
1676 - 1761

Anna Walraven
died @ 1713

Nils Lycon
1666 - 1721

Maria Gastenberg
died after 1732

Christopher Springer
1593 - 1669

Beata Henrickson Salina
died 1693

Hendrick Jacobsson

Gertrude

Robert Robinson

(unknown)

Walraven Jansen de Vos

Christina Ollesdotter

Peter Nilsson Lycon

(unknown)

Ollie Nielson Gastenberg

Cecilia

WESLEY BURNETT
1818 – 1905

Wesley Burnett was born January 4, 1818 in a log cabin built by his father on the family farm in Sullivan County, Indiana. The town of New Lebanon has since been built near the original Burnett farm. This area is located in southwestern Indiana, near the east bank of the Wabash River, and some twenty-five miles south of Terre Haute, Indiana. His father was William Burnett and his mother was Mary Springer Burnett. His parents were married about 1800 in Kentucky, and soon after moved to the wilds of Indiana. Many of the events of Wesley's young life, and the conditions under which he was raised, have been covered in his parent's biographical chapters of the Burnett Family History.

His childhood was typical to that of the other children raised on the frontier. He did not have a pair of pants until he was twelve years old; he wore a long shirt or gown, spun by his mother. It was his only garment. Wesley fished in the streams near the farm for catfish, which were plentiful. He plowed the corn, when he was too small to reach the plow handles, by grasping the plow rounds that stabilized those handles.

At five years of age he professed Christ. Near the farm was a camp where a black preacher held a series of meetings. Wesley was converted and joined the Methodist Church, to which he remained devoted for the rest of his life.

In time, a school was established in the settlement. The teacher kept a bundle of switches on his desk, and one day when Wesley did something contrary to the rules, he was chastised. The teacher took the bundle of switches by the small ends and hit Wesley on the side of the face with the butt ends. As a result of this incident he quit school, with the consent of his parents, and did not return until they got a new teacher.

As a young man, Wesley attended Asbury University at Green Castle, Indiana. After attending there two years, he went into business and taught school at the same time. Because of the increased activity of his business, he soon gave up teaching. He was out to make his fortune.

For a time, he ran a sawmill on his father's farm. The power was supplied by oxen working in a treadmill. This gave Wesley an idea. If he could take some of this lumber and make flatboats to float the rivers he could go into the shipping business. This he did, putting the rough planks together with hickory pins. After his first boat was launched, he loaded it with produce, which was principally corn grown at the settlement. Then with a small crew of men, he bade farewell to his family. By floating down the Rolling Fork, and then the Wabash River, Wesley could reach the Ohio River and then the Mississippi for the float, with his cargo, to New Orleans. There he sold his cargo, as well as the boat itself. The timbers were cut into lumber at a Louisiana sawmill. It was a profitable business. In one season he built three flatboats and floated them as a flotilla all the way to New Orleans. One of these flatboats was the largest ever taken down the Rolling Fork River to the Mississippi.

Wesley Burnett was in this business for nine years, from 1840 until 1849. On one of these trips a severe epidemic of cholera broke out along the lower Mississippi River, all the way to the gulf at New Orleans. Wesley talked to a doctor, before floating into the infected area, and received a remedy for treating the disease. Shortly thereafter, he got a call from one of the boats that one of the crew members had come down with the cholera. Wesley immediately gave orders to tie the crafts to the trees along the river so he could treat the ill man. As soon as the first boat was made fast to the shore, the settlers cut the boat loose. They didn't want any diseased people on their land! With that, Wesley worked his boat alongside, and jumped over to treat the sick man. The remedy proved to be effective, as the crewman soon recovered.

It was a frightening experience for all who plied the Mississippi in those years, for the dead from the cholera were everywhere. Wesley tells of seeing the dead bodies floating in the river. Out of fear, the diseased were tossed overboard. It was reported, "Rough river men quit swearing, and took to praying and singing hymns." During this time, Wesley's boats passed a steam-driven paddle boat tied to a dock, on which a number of corpses were laying there on the deck. It was on this trip that a neighbor, who lived near the Burnett Ranch in Indiana, returned home from his trip on the river, and reported, "Wesley is surely dead from the cholera!" It proved to be a case of mistaken identity, which caused Wesley's father and mother needless sorrow. The truth was, Wesley was one of the most successful riverboat operators on the

Mississippi. He never lost a man during the nine-year operation, and he built up a small fortune during that period of time.

While in New Orleans, Wesley Burnett came in contact with one of the most revolting features of slavery. It was the selling and buying of slaves. To see the heartbreak of families being torn apart as they were sold off to the slave owners broke Wesley's heart, too. Up until that time he had been a registered Democrat, as were his parents. The Burnetts were Jacksonian Democrats. But over the issue of slavery, which came to a head when Kansas was brought into the Union as a free state, they became Republicans. When the Democrats continued to support slavery, Wesley was livid! He remained a Republican for the rest of his life, but at times in his later years he sometimes voted the Prohibition Party ticket. The family had a long history of opposition to the use of alcohol. They had seen the hardship, sorrow, and tragedy which "booze" had brought to the frontier. Wesley's father, William Burnett, was the first leader in Indiana to banish whiskey from "log rollings and huskings."

*　　　　　*　　　　　*

With the exciting news of the gold discovery of 1849 in California, Wesley Burnett immediately began making plans for the great adventure which would take him west. He had built up considerable capital for the move, something over five-thousand dollars, from his flat-boating business. Once his intentions became known in New Lebanon, many of the young men implored Wesley to take them with him. After all, he had the resources to equip the endeavor, and he was a proven leader.

Finally, nine young men were selected. All had made a firm commitment. It was this: "Wesley would provide transportation and supplies to take them to California. In return, they would give Wesley one-half of what they made during the first three years in the gold fields." The proposition sounded good. Of course they all expected to get rich in a very short time. So, Wesley accepted their promissory commitment and immediately set about getting ready for the trip.

He rigged up a six-mule team, two ox-teams, and several yoke of spare oxen for each wagon. The spare oxen would be added insurance if any of the stock became incapacitated on the long and difficult journey. All of this preparation was done in the winter of 1849-1850. Then in the spring of 1850, they bid goodbye to their families and friends, and places of their youth--all of which they would never see again. Their loved ones watched with heavy heart, as the white covered wagons slowly moved out of sight.

This was a particularly hard time for Wesley's mother, Mary Springer Burnett. She knew she would never see her son again. "Be faithful to God," she admonished. "We will meet in heaven." There is no doubt that the influence of his mother's and father's intense religious zeal and strong faith in God saved Wesley from the ruin which engulfed so many of the gold hunters.

Once out on the Great Plains, with civilization behind them, tensions began to grow within the party. Even the normally gentle oxen became wild. They would stretch their heads up, sniffing the air as if they smelled danger. At night the men belled the oxen, so they could keep track of the animals. One night some of the oxen took fright and stampeded. As quickly as possible, Wesley followed them on horseback. The sound of the bells grew fainter and finally ceased. The men hunted and hunted their lost stock, but they never saw them again. Whether they took fright from wild animals or Indians stole them, they never knew. The loss certainly put a severe handicap on the expedition, but because Wesley had planned for such a possibility, the party moved on without further delay.

Like so many others, they were bothered with bowel trouble throughout the journey. At times, what seemed to be a mild type of cholera hit the group. However, none of Wesley's men died on the journey.

At certain points along the way, where there was good water and grass for the stock, the wagons would stop over for several days. There they would rest and recuperate. At one of these camps, the men tried out a new long-range rifle. It was a firearm specially crafted to be taken across the plains and the mountains to California. He called the rifle his "baby cannon."

The range at which they were shooting was two-hundred yards. The target was a small piece of white paper on a stake. Several shots were taken, but no one hit the mark. At this point, Wesley came along, picked up the rifle, and shot at the target offhand. At the crack of the gun, the paper mark dropped. He had hit it dead center. Then without saying a word, Wesley laid the gun down and walked away. "That Burnett is sure a dead shot," one of the men remarked. Wesley carried that reputation throughout the duration of his life.

There is a place along the wagon trail to California called Rattlesnake Butte. When the wagon train camped there, Wesley climbed the butte to survey the land ahead. It was dusk. Right under his feet he heard the alarming buzz of a rattlesnake! He jumped back, only to hear the rattle of another snake. Then another snake joined the growing chorus. All of a sudden, the evening air became filled with their incessant buzzing. Wesley had stumbled into a rattlesnake den. With alacrity, powered by some feeling of danger, Wesley jumped back down the rocks to safety.

The trail took them through South Pass, a twenty-mile-wide high rolling plain opening, which broke the barrier of the Rocky Mountains, and then on to Fort Bridger. The passage of late spring and early summer across the great plains of Nebraska and the high grass lands of Wyoming had not been without incidents. From one camp the cattle had strayed away. Wesley again took up the search. He climbed a small hill to get a better view. Off in the sagebrush he caught sight of a number of Indians traveling in single file across the country. Wesley backed off and lay hidden in the high grass until the Indians had passed.

There were two other incidents with the Indians, as the wagon train made its way west, both of which illustrate the potential for tragic conflict in these crossings. Many such incidents were initiated by the Argonauts (i.e., those going to California to seek gold after the 1849 discovery) and the pioneers themselves. It is reassuring to find that Burnett opposed both actions, in which the wagon train he was traveling was involved. These incidents are reviewed, because it is important for future generations to have perspective on our ancestor's part in these tragic events.

Here is the first incident. Wesley Burnett's wagon train witnessed one of the most tragic incidents that ever took place on the plains. A number of traveling parties were camped along the river at the same place on this particular evening. A young man, who was a member of one of the other parties on the journey, declared, "I'm going to kill the first Indian I see." Several weeks later, he saw an Indian sitting on a log, fishing near the place where Wesley and his men had camped. This young man, whom Wesley did not know, picked up his rifle and shot the Indian, only to find that the Indian was a squaw.

The next morning the camp was surrounded by several hundred armed Indians. They explained that one of their squaws had been killed by a white man. "Give us the guilty one," they declared! "You either give him to us or we will kill you all."

The white men held a parley. They decided to fight it out with the Indians. At this point, the guilty man stepped forward and said, "I don't want to be responsible for any more deaths." With that, he surrendered to the Indians, who proceeded to string him to a tree. There, in full view of the entire camp, the Indians skinned the young man alive. All watched his painful death.

On occasion, this story was told by members of our family. As a small boy, it disturbed my sleep on many nights. Years later I found this tragedy also repeated in some of the histories of the California trail.

The second incident with the Indians occurred after Wesley and his men reached the grassy meadows of the Humboldt River, near present day Lovelock, Nevada. The wagon trains stopped there to feed their stock, preparatory to making the dry, hot run across the alkali sinks. Here in the desert heat, the Humboldt River disappeared.

While Wesley was camped at Big Meadow a man by the name of Burnett, from one of the other wagon trains, reported, "The Indians have stolen my cattle!" He was endeavoring to raise a company to go out and recover his stock and punish the Indians. This Burnett was no relation to Wesley. In fact he was a complete stranger. Wesley said, "It's a fool-hardy thing to do!" But several members of his own wagon train taunted him, "You are a coward, and afraid to go!"

If there was one thing Wesley Burnett was not, it was a coward. He always went where duty called, regardless of the danger. In fact he did not seem to know what fear was. Despite his better judgment, he replied, "Very well. If you put in on that ground, we will join the fight."

There were twenty men in the expedition. A man named Walker was elected captain and Wesley took charge of his own men under Walker. They made their way up a creek that ran into the Humboldt River. After riding for about thirty miles, they approached the encampment of the Indians under the cover of chaparral and rough terrain. It was a surprise attack!

The Indians scattered under the initial assault, but not without first grabbing their guns and jumping on their horses. The Indians realized they greatly outnumbered the attacking white men and they organized to fight. Wesley remembers, "There must have been three-hundred mounted Indians with guns, galloping around us. The whooping braves would conceal their bodies behind their horses. It was amazing how they could get a shot off at us over the back or under the neck of their horses on the full run. It became apparent that our small group was in a serious situation!"

One of Wesley's men, who had a fine saddle horse, and who had been one of the most eager to join the expedition, kept yelling, "For God's sake, let's stop shooting and get out of here!" The safety of the camp, some thirty miles away, looked mighty good to him just then.

Wesley Burnett was over six-foot tall, and in this fight he wore a red shirt, brown pants and a white Panama hat. This made him a conspicuous target. Several times during the fight he saw an Indian rise up out of the grass and fire his rifle. Each time he heard the lead ball whistle past his head. The Indians evidently took him for the captain, because of his distinctive dress. Wesley could never fire back at the Indian, because he was armed with a double-barrel shotgun loaded with buckshot. The Indian, with his rifle, was out of range.

It was amazing; the Indians were better armed than the whites. After the fight had been in progress about an hour, Walker held a consultation with Wesley. "What is the best thing to do?" Walker asked.

Wesley replied, "There is only one thing to do. Fall back in order and fire as we go!" This was carried out successfully. The Indians followed them for a short distance and then disappeared. Burnett, with the other men, began the long trip back to their camp, tired but a little wiser. Little did they know that the Indians in the meantime had regrouped with reinforcements and were cutting across country to intercept them for another engagement. But good fortune was still with Wesley. When they arrived back at Big Meadow they found, since they had left, several other trains had come in. As Wesley and his men arrived, a scout came galloping into camp. He was pursued by a band of Indians in war paint on their fleet ponies.

The wagons were quickly circled in a roughly rectangular configuration, and the Argonauts prepared for battle. There were about 600 Indians in the war party. Whooping it up, they galloped around the wagons. The Indian leaders, after seeing the fortification and arms of the wagon trains, decided not to attack and rode away. The fact that a number of wagon trains, by chance, had come together at the Meadows, before crossing the Humboldt Sink, undoubtedly saved these parties from massacre. It was a secure feeling for all the tired travelers to camp together during this time of threat and danger.

That night the men discussed the encounter with the raiding Indians. Some said they had seen several Indians fall during the fight, and they were certain quite a few were killed. But Wesley said, "I did not see a single Indian fall and I do not believe there was a single Indian killed or wounded. It was just a lot of shooting and noise." However, there was no doubt; the Indians had been stirred up. They were Shoshone Indians and they had tried to defend their lands along this section of the trail for many years. Although these wagon trains got off well, many that followed paid dearly for the folly of this attack. The Indians, to the surprise of many, had guns. It was illegal to sell guns to Indians. This illicit trade for profit became a growing problem for the families crossing the continent. Finally, just prior to the Civil War, the U.S. Army convoyed the wagon trains through this portion of the California Trail.

*   *   *

Finally, this great meadow area, with its abundant feed and water, would be left behind. Ahead lay the most treacherous part of the entire trip: the Humboldt Sink crossing. The dreaded Humboldt Sink was a desolate alkaline desert into which the Humboldt River disappeared. The cattle and mules were still worn out from the toiling journey from the Wabash River far away. Emigrants were forced to lighten their loads. Everything not absolutely necessary had to be thrown away, if they were to have a successful crossing. So

71

Wesley, confronted with the same necessity that confronted all the other emigrants, ordered the wagons lightened. "Boys, throw out everything that is not absolutely necessary for the rest of the trip. Keep only the things we can't get along without. It's getting late. Snow will soon be falling in the Sierra, and we don't want to get caught up there in the mountains. This is a tough crossing coming up. Let's get on with it!" Such were Wesley's orders to his crew. They were meant both as a demand to unload and an encouragement for the perilous pull across the desert ahead. The boys threw out all unnecessary luggage and the wagons proceeded with a lightened load.

A day later, while the train was halted for the noon rest, Wesley noticed two of his men carrying a large trunk that they had picked up by the side of the trail. Wesley saw them sneaking it to the back of one of the wagons. Wesley confronted them. "What are you doing?" He said this with some irritation.

"Well," replied one of the men, "my things have been kicking around long enough, and I'm going to put them in the trunk."

"You needn't bother yourself. Just leave the trunk on the ground," Wesley replied. With that the man flew into a terrible rage, and wound up saying, "Wesley, I'll have your life blood before we reach California." But he did leave the trunk in the desert.

Unfortunately, this type of tension-filled incident was not unusual on the wagon trains traveling west. Emotions often ran high, and cussedness and rebellion were daily dangers faced by the wagon masters. Wesley, too, became exasperated at times. He saw his boys develop traits of meanness and cussedness during the journey. Experienced wagon masters predicted it, but still it was hard for Wesley to believe it could happen in his crew. He said many years later, "If I had not promised their parents, before starting the trip, that I would take them safely to California, I would have taken my mules, my wagons, and my nephews, and let the neighbor boys fend for themselves with their ox-team. I could have cut several weeks off our travel time and eliminated a lot of the problems."

After the heat, alkali, and thirst of the arid Humboldt Sink, came the clear waters of the Truckee River. "It was amazing," Wesley's son, J. K. Burnett, wrote many years later. "They came up over this rolling ridge at the west end of the Sink. There below was the clear water of the Truckee River, flowing through a gentle turn to the north—right out there in the middle of those barren and rocky hills! The dashing pure water gave the men and stock alike new life. They paused. The great blue barrier of the Sierra Nevada Mountains loomed ahead—the last great obstacle of their trip."

On they pushed. And then on a bright afternoon, in October 1850, the wagons worked their way around the glacial-rounded granite boulders, many towering higher than the covered wagons, and reached the summit. They paused. Spread out before these hardy adventurers was the land of their dreams: California. His son later wrote, "What pen can describe the thrill of the moment? It was purchased at a price of toil, privation and danger. To fully understand, an adventure such as this can only be experienced."

It was downhill now, all the way to Sacramento. In a few days their battered train pulled into that rushing, roaring town, the embarkation center for the gold-mining boom. Wesley's party broke up and hustled to the diggings before the blast of winter set in. As for Wesley, he first secured pasture for his depleted animals, and stored his wagons for future use. Then he and his nephews went off on a scouting mission for the streams where gold ore might be found. When Wesley found a possible location, he provided the boys with the picks, shovels, pans, and rockers needed for the mining operation. Then he would move on, locating other possible areas to lay claim.

After several days Wesley returned to check on the boys' progress. William Burnett, his nephew, spoke up, "There is no use in working here. I haven't found gold enough to make wages."

Wesley replied, "Well, it seems to all be a gamble anyway. I want to check it out anyway, and this is as good as any place to dig." With that he began to work. In his last shovel of gravel, at the bottom of his hole, Wesley saw the flash of gold! Reaching into the water he drew out a large bright nugget, and threw it into the rocker for all to see. It showed bright in the sunlight. Miners working along the creek came running to see the astounding nugget. There was great excitement. All began digging again with frenzy, but no more rich nuggets were found. Wages could be made, if one worked long hours in the cold water, but that did not satisfy the wild seekers of sudden wealth.

Then there came a rumor that at Rich Bar on the Sacramento River a great strike had been made, "Gold is being taken out by the tub full!" With that, all the miners took off. They carried what equipment they could on their backs and left the rest. But Rich Bar proved to be no better than their original claims. Wesley and his nephews continued to join the rushes to the new reported areas of rich strikes, but they were always disappointed. Wesley made nothing more than wages.

There was irony in the adventure. After Wesley abandoned his original claim, a New York man landed from a steamer in San Francisco, and immediately went to the gold fields. He began his dig in the same hole where Wesley had found the gold nugget. He dug a few more feet and struck a reef of rocks. He continued digging behind this reef, and there he found the bedrock lined with coarse gold. During that winter of 1850-1851, with pick, pan, and rocker, the man took out over seventy-thousand dollars in gold. With that, at the end of four months, he returned to New York with his newfound wealth.

The spring of 1851 found Wesley thoroughly disgusted with mining. He decided to take up teaming. He broke up the mining relationship with his nephews, got his faithful mules and wagons, and began a freight service between Sacramento and the various mining camps in the Sierra.

On one of his return trips from the mines, one of the boys, who had come with Wesley to California, asked if he could ride with him to Sacramento. Upon their arrival they unhitched and fed the team. Then they went to the Old Eldorado, a famous gambling resort, for a little entertainment. Gambling games of all kinds were "running high." At one table sat a man far gone with liquor. The table was piled high with gold, and he was playing his cards in a very reckless manner. "Let's play. It'll be easy to win some money from him," said the young miner with Wesley.

"Keep away from that kind of game," Wesley heeded. But the warning was not heeded and the young man put his sack of gold dust on the table. The gambler threw out the cards, and turned up the winning number. Instead of paying off his lost bet, the young miner grabbed his bag of gold and rushed for the door.

Wesley, realizing immediately that such action would bring death to his companion, grabbed the boy before he got out the door. Half-dozen pistols were pointed at them. The gamblers declared that they had both attempted to escape without paying the bet. Wesley had great difficulty in convincing them that he had grabbed the young man to prevent him from running out on the debt. Finally, the gamblers became satisfied Wesley was honest. With that, they put up their pistols, settled the debt, and got on with their game. It had been a close call! The boy went back to the mines, a poorer but wiser lad, thanks to Wesley Burnett. It is said, "Every foot of the floor of the Old Eldorado was, at one time or another, stained with human blood."

This ended the gold rush experiences of Wesley Burnett. Only one of the boys who came with Wesley to California ever made good on the original agreement. This one boy was his nephew, William Burnett, who gave Wesley six-hundred dollars of the twelve-hundred dollars he made in the mines.

*   *   *

In the fall of 1851, Wesley decided to try farming. He formed a partnership with a man named Shetzer. Together, they went to Santa Clara Valley, and acquired one hundred twenty acres of land, where the town of Santa Clara now stands. The ranch belonged to Wesley Burnett, but the partners worked it together on shares. They planted eighty acres in wheat, barley and potatoes. Wesley could load a thousand dollars worth of potatoes on one of his freight wagons, and then sell them in a day. He was always paid in full with gold. All the crops did well. The first year they sold twenty-thousand dollars worth of produce. This was a considerable amount of money in those days.

Burnett and Shetzer then purchased a mowing machine, at a cost of eight-hundred dollars. The equipment had come by sailing ship around Cape Horn, the southern tip of South America. Wesley then constructed an innovative and ingenious contraption for thrashing the grain. It was like a large sieve, woven with strips of rawhide and close enough together to hold the straw. The grain, when beaten against the posts, would then fall through the openings. This was the way they thrashed the wheat, the first ever raised in the Santa Clara Valley, and some of the first in California. The grain, too, was in great demand, providing a valued source of further income. Wesley soon planted an orchard, and built a comfortable house on his ranch.

When the Methodist Church needed land to build a school, he donated ten acres. This is how it happened. About 1852, Wesley's brother-in-law, Reverend N.P. Heath and his sister, Cynthia (Burnett) Heath, came from the east across the Panama Isthmus and lived with him for a while at the ranch. Rev. Heath was a Methodist preacher and organized the first Methodist Church in Santa Clara. The Methodist Church had established a school in Sonoma County, north of the San Francisco Bay area, but desired to expand it into a college, and locate it in a more central area.

They selected Santa Clara as the suitable place to establish the new college. Reverend Heath and Cynthia (Burnett) Heath were leaders in the negotiations. To seal the deal, Wesley deeded the Methodist Church ten acres of his ranch, upon which to build the buildings for the new college. From this start emerged the College of the Pacific, the first privately-funded college in the State of California. My mother, Hope Gould Robinson, graduated from the College of the Pacific in 1915, when it was still located in the Santa Clara Valley.

*   *   *

About 1855, Wesley sold his Santa Clara ranch, and purchased a saw mill on Soquel Creek near Santa Cruz. The sawmill was located two or three miles up the creek from the small town of Soquel. The mill consisted of one circular saw and one upright saw. The steady oxen driven across the plains were used in logging for the mill.

It was while running this mill that Wesley met Mary Kennedy Cooper. Mary was a widow and a teacher in Santa Cruz. Her first husband had tragically disappeared, and was later pronounced dead, leaving Mary with two small boys. Wesley was immediately attracted to Mary and, shortly after, they were married. The details of this episode in their lives are further covered in the story of Mary Burnett.

In 1859, Wesley sold his sawmill, and moved to northern San Luis Obispo County to fulfill his dream. He had always wanted to develop an extensive cattle ranch. Wesley was soon established on his new homestead, located on the south side of the Nacimiento, about four miles west of where the Las Tablos River joins the Nacimiento River. This area is some eighteen miles northwest of Paso Robles, California. In the next forty-six years, until his death in 1905, Wesley Burnett lived in a half dozen places on the vast ranches he developed from Paso Robles to the Pacific Ocean, north of Cayucos, California. Some of the events of these years are chronicled in the chapters on his wife, Mary Kennedy Burnett, and his oldest daughter, Rosamond Burnett Robinson. These stories, along with the incidents now recorded in Wesley's history in San Luis Obispo County, provide a valued account of this period and of his memorable life.

*   *   *

Soon after his arrival at the Nacimiento, in 1859, Wesley built a log cabin, a log barn, and adjoining corrals to hold the stock. He bought several hundred head of cattle and ran them on the government range. Actually, settlers at the time were little more than squatters. They would find a piece of unoccupied land, where water was available, "prove it up" a bit, and then call it "my ranch." The other settlers would respect that right. That's how the Burnett ranch got started in this area,

In 1860, there were only two families who had settled in northern San Luis Obispo County. One was Wesley Burnett, and the other was the James Lynch family, who had settled some four miles upstream from the Burnett's, and on the other side of the Nacimiento River. The two families became good friends and supported each other through difficult times that were ahead.

There were many grizzly bears along the Nacimiento during those early years. To protect the cattle, Wesley hunted the marauding bears with a muzzle loading rifle. These rifles could only get off one shot at a time. With this weapon and a large knife, he would hunt. The technique was to select a bluff overlooking the river. There he would wait for a grizzly to appear. The river bottoms were a favorite place to attack the cattle, when they came to drink.

Wesley had several close calls with the bears. One time he fell asleep while on watch. All of a sudden, he was awaked by a large bear that came up behind him. The grizzly reared with his fore legs extended above his head. It was a fear-filled moment! Wesley rose to a crouched position, got off the one shot he had, and hit the animal in the chest. The bear thrashed the brush and then fell dead at Wesley's feet.

Wesley Burnett brought the first bees to the Nacimiento country. He brought the first few hives from Santa Cruz. Soon after, bees became plentiful in San Luis Obispo County.

We know that sometime during these years, Wesley leased a portion of the Piedra Blanca Rancho from a Spaniard by the name of Juan Castro. This is important because, through this relationship, Wesley Burnett would become the future owner of the Geronimo Grant at Cayucos. We know that during the early 1860's, Wesley was actively engaged in the Piedra Blanca Rancho, on which the Hearst Castle above San Simeon, California is located today. Even now, top geographical features of the area carry the Wesley Burnett name: Burnett Creek, Little Burnett Creek, and Burnett Peak. All of these are reminders of this pioneer in those early days.

The ranch became productive. By 1864, Wesley was running a thousand head of cattle on the ranch and the adjacent rangeland. Then the great California drought came. The land became blistered and parched as day after day the hot sun burned the earth. There was no grass and the cattle died by the thousands all over the state. Wesley watched his herds die, as the streams and springs dried up and the feed vanished. Only three prize heifers, out of the hundred he had purchased the year before, lived through the spring of 1865. The cattle that survived took to the high mountains of the coastal range and became wild.

When the drought was over, the farmers in the area joined forces to recover what cattle they could find. The plan was for the cowhands to round up some of the tamer cows, then work this stock until they could drive and hold them in place. This required patience, careful work, and ingenuity on the part of the cowboys. Then, when they located the wild cattle, which had fled to the high Santa Lucia Mountains for feed, the men drove the tamer herds as near to the wild cattle as possible. Some of the cowboys remained to guard the cattle in the tamer herd, while the others worked around the wild cattle, and then ran them back into the tame herd. Once the two herds joined, it was possible to join them with another wild bunch of cattle.

The cowboys worked this way for months, constantly increasing the herd of now gentler cattle. At the end of the roundup, each cowman could then drive his own stock home. They were sorry little herds in comparison to the large well-nourished cattle they had in the fall of 1863. The drought of 1864 left

Wesley with less than one hundred head of cattle, out of a herd of a thousand he had the year before. This discouraged him from continuing his cattle business in the Adelaida area.

The coastal section of the county received more rain, so there he would establish a new ranch. He was a man who did not tarry. That fall, 1865, he took his family, stock, and belongings to Villa Creek, some twelve miles north of Cayucos.

It is interesting to note here that Wesley and Mary Burnett, before leaving their Nacimiento Homestead, gave their home, barns and land to their friends James and Alice Lynch.

Wesley believed Villa Creek was government land, open for settlement. It didn't work out that way. Not long after moving to Villa Creek, Pedro Marques and Santiago Hernandez claimed the land was theirs. Wesley paid them six-hundred dollars for a quit claim deed. A later survey showed that the land actually was a part of the Geronimo grant, so Wesley lost out again. To make matters worse, before Wesley and the family could move, a California storm hit the area, flooding all that Wesley had built in the fall. The storm wrecked the ranch, drowned the chickens and some the stock, and some of the hogs were swept down Villa Creek into the sea.

Wesley's oldest son, J. K. Burnett, many years later wrote, "Villa Creek became a roaring torrent, perhaps fifteen-feet deep. Father dug holes under the log foundations of the house to let some of the water run through, hoping this would keep our house from washing away. For a night and a day the stream roared. We didn't get much sleep!"

The month of May, 1866, was a time of great uncertainty, readjustment, and emerging hope for the Burnett family. Juan Jose Castro, the Spaniard who had leased Wesley the north portion of the Pedro Blanca Rancho, came to Villa Creek. He proposed to sell the Burnetts his property, which was south of Villa Creek and the northern part of the famous Geronimo Grant. This was a beautiful three-thousand acre tract of land on the coast. "I can't buy your place," Wesley told Castro. "It's impossible! How could I buy such a place? I have very little money now, and very little stock."

"I'll sell it to you on credit," said Castro. He was determined Wesley should buy the property, so determined that he stayed with the Burnett family for a couple of weeks, helping them with the work. He was very helpful and agreeable, all the time talking to Wesley about buying the ranch. He told Wesley, "I have no stock on the place, and not enough money to pay the taxes." Wesley and Mary Burnett consented to buy the ranch. The deed was recorded on May 26, 1866.

There was a house on the place. It was located in a shallow draw, a little over a mile from the ocean, and about a mile and a half north of Cayucos. Other than the house, there were no improvements on the place. The price for the 3,000 acres was $3,600, $1,315 in cash and Castro took a mortgage on the balance. This proved to be the most fortunate business transaction of Wesley and Mary Burnett's life. As far as they were concerned, it had come as a "Gift from God," and at a very low point in their lives. They called their new land Coast Ranch.

What cattle, horses, and hogs they had left were moved to the coast place, which was about seven miles south of the Villa Creek ranch. All the stock was moved to Coast Ranch, before the Burnett family actually made their own move. With the massive rains of the winter and early spring, the rolling country had sprung alive with a towering crop of wild oats, which soon dried in the early summer. A great fire exploded in the rolling hills. Fortunately, there was plenty of warning, for the smoke could be seen several days before it reached the Coast Ranch.

There the dirt road cut through the ranch about a hundred yards from the ocean. Wesley, and the boys, rounded up the cattle and hogs and drove them to the portion of the ranch that ran between the road and the beach. Wesley then backfired along the inland side of the road. The sea breeze took the flames away. This saved the animals from the roaring fire, which at times moved as fast as a horse could run. With the grass all burned off, what was to become of the stock? As a matter of fact, they did better after the fire than before. The oat seeds had dropped out of the oat heads and lay in handfuls on the ground. The fire had moved so fast, it had only scorched the grain, creating a better feed for both hogs and cattle than before the fire.

The rains came again. He stocked new herds of cattle, flocks of sheep, and within three years raised enough hogs to drive them to market at San Francisco; a feat defying imagination. There he sold the hogs for enough money to pay off the mortgage on the Coast Ranch.

We are not certain as to when or under what circumstances he sold the Coast Ranch and returned to Adelaida. In 1875 he was a registered voter at Morro Bay, which was the polling place for the Cayucos area, and yet his son, William Burnett, was born at Adelaida in 1872. One thing is clear, history records: "In the 1870's, Wesley Burnett returned to the Adelaida area and started acquiring large ranch holdings, about 20,000 acres by 1890. Of these, 16,000 were around Adelaida, 2,000 in the Whitley Gardens area, and another 2,000 acres in the Cholame Valley, twenty miles east of Paso Robles."

During this exciting time of land expansion, Wesley became more and more concerned over the failing health of his beloved wife. Mary Kennedy

Burnett lived out her last years at Rancho de los Mulos. When she died on January 20, 1878, at the age of forty-eight, the family was devastated. Mary had been the steadying influence on Wesley and a loving partner upon whom he depended. Now he was left alone with five children, all under sixteen years of age. The light had gone out of his life.

High on the oak ridge across from the house, Mary was lovingly put to rest; the first to ever be buried on what later became the Adelaida Cemetery. From the house, Wesley would look up and see the stone pillar that marked her grave.

The story of how Wesley increased his holdings in the years between 1865 and 1885 is a fascinating one. My father, Franklin W. Robinson, a grandson of Wesley Burnett, told me, "Grandfather Burnett would put up a small down payment on a piece of property, and pay some of it off in the good years. Whenever a settler fell on hard times, he could go to Grandfather and receive cash for the property. When Grandfather Burnett received the money from the sale, he would refinance and buy up more property, until he owned ranches from the coast at Cayucos, to Paso Robles, and on east to the Cholame Valley. In this way he built up control of all this beautiful rangeland. At the height of these acquisitions, he had 40,000 sheep and large herds of cattle. To my knowledge he never gambled at cards or other games of chance, but he played for high stakes in business dealings."

After his wife Mary Kennedy died, Wesley continued to involve himself in land acquisition. He was sufficiently well-off to send all of his surviving five children to the University of Southern California; quite an accomplishment in those times. It is interesting to note that all three of his girls, Rosamond, Helen, and Lillie, married classmates at USC. His boys, James and William, also attended USC, but later graduated from Stanford University with law degrees. His youngest boy, William, after a sixteen month deployment in the Philippines during the Spanish American War, returned to Stanford. There he was captain of the football team and president of his class.

James (J.K.), Wesley's oldest son, entered law practice in San Luis Obispo. During this time, he also served in the State Legislature, where he became a champion of the common man and fought the tycoons of the time.

Wesley continued with his ranch operations. Most of his energy, however, went into developing his special piece of property, the 320-acre homestead, Rancho de los Mulos at Nacimiento. A reporter from the San Luis Obispo Tribune visited Rancho de los Mulos on May 22, 1885. He wrote:

Arrived at W. W. Burnett's and was surprised to find a mountain ranch that compared favorably with the best farms in this county. The ranch

is known everywhere as the Corral de los Mulos, and is owned by Wesley Burnett. The soil is black and strong. Water is abundant and improvements are good. They consist of good fencing, a large barn, a granary, which is large, trim, and strong, and a dwelling house that's a hundred feet long. It bespeaks the hospitality of the occupants. In a word, this ranch will hardly be surpassed anywhere.

Mr. Burnett is quite proud of this farm and it would take a handsome price to relieve him of it. Mr. Burnett has speculated heavily in lands on this side of the mountain, and will no doubt reap a much deserved golden harvest from these lands in the near future.

Unfortunately, Wesley had become overextended. He was forced to gradually liquidate his holdings to pay off his creditors. By the time the panic of the late 1890's was over, all that Wesley had left, from his vast holdings, was Rancho de los Mulos. Then on March 9, 1901, the <u>Paso Robles Record</u> reported, "Last Saturday night the farmhouse of Wesley Burnett burned to the ground."

In the last years of his life, Wesley Burnett suffered. On July 10, 1905, he died. These are excerpts from the obituary published in the <u>Paso Robles Daily News</u>:

… Wesley Burnett had a truly remarkable life. He quietly passed away from senile debility … The deceased was well known throughout this county, where he formerly held great land interests … He was respected and honored for his honesty and good will by all who knew him … Wesley Burnett was laid to rest in the Adelaida Cemetery, next to his beloved wife, Mary Kennedy Burnett.

In later years, Wesley's grave was marked only by a small block of cement, unlettered and void of identification. Then in 2001, his great-granddaughter, Louise Holler Craddock, and her husband Sheldon, placed, at the Nacimiento Cemetery, an engraved headstone on the grave of Wesley Burnett.

Not only did Wesley have a "truly remarkable life," he led a complex one as well. In seeking an authenticity for his biography, it is necessary to explore some of these complexities. Most can be recognized as character strengths. But as can happen, God-given strengths, when out of balance, can become debilitating weaknesses. Here are four apparent strengths; strengths which members of future generations might wish to examine, as they deal with their own inherited genes. One studies history to understand the present.

- Wesley Burnett had an inner drive for adventure.

Few men who settled the West experienced more adventure. Wesley successfully negotiated his flatboats, loaded with timber and goods, the length of the Mississippi River. He did this successfully time after time, and under the most perilous of conditions. He successfully led a well-organized wagon train across the continent to the California gold fields, confronting the challenges of the plains, marauding Indians, a perilous desert and the rugged Sierra. He searched unsuccessfully for gold. He built a fortune as a farmer, as a sawmill operator, as a pioneer settler and as a developer in one of the most valued and beautiful areas of California.

- Wesley Burnett had a heart of generosity.

In reviewing the life of Wesley Burnett, one can only be impressed with his generous spirit. Few men would have taken on the responsibility of his neighbors' boys on the perilous journey to California in the search for gold. Later he gave a portion of his farm in Santa Clara to the Methodist Church to establish the College of Pacific, the first private college in the State of California. Too, have we ever heard of a pioneer family giving their homestead to a friend and neighbor? While living on the Coast Ranch at Cayucos, he gave his finest horse to a Methodist circuit rider, to carry on the ministry. Even in 1889, when in deep financial trouble, Wesley gave land to build the Tablos School in Nacimiento, and a beautiful seven acres of his Rancho Corral de los Mulos to the Methodist Episcopal Church, and the site of the Nacimiento Cemetery. He built a town meeting hall on his land for the use of Methodist evangelical camp meetings, and gave a generous tithe to the various Methodist churches he attended from San Luis Obispo to Nacimiento. Wesley saw himself as a steward for all the Lord had provided.

- Wesley Burnett had an active spiritual dimension.

One cannot review the life of Wesley Burnett without detecting the spiritual foundation upon which his life was built. It came ingrained from his devoted parents, William and Mary Springer Burnett, intrepid pioneers of the Indiana territory. The Burnetts were a God-fearing family. As Indiana grew, they desired to have the gospel preached in their area. William had heard that a Methodist preacher was holding services in Kentucky, so he mounted his horse and rode down into Kentucky and located the preacher. As a small boy,

Wesley remembers when the new pastor came to his parents' home for the first services. Many years after, Wesley Burnett as a grown young man sawed the timber to build the first church in Sullivan County, Indiana.

Wesley never lost his faith. He carried it west, where his beliefs sustained him through the founding of a new land. Prayer, commitment, and Christian discipleship were only strengthened through his marriage to Mary Kennedy Burnett. Prayer was a significant part of their life together.

Wesley and Mary Burnett were charter members of the Methodist Church in San Luis Obispo, California. They faithfully made the twenty-five mile wagon trip from Cayucos to San Luis Obispo to attend church. Wesley never wore Christianity on his sleeve. It was in his heart. Traveling circuit riders sought the Burnetts for lodging and hospitality. New Christian schools, from the College of Pacific, to the new University of Southern California, asked and received Wesley's support.

Wesley Burnett had witnessed the destruction of human life on the frontier by the whiskey trade. For a time he voted the Prohibition Party ticket. But in the end, he knew the solution for problems of morality came through a change of heart. Many lives were saved in the Methodist camp meetings held on his land.

- <u>Wesley Burnett was a restless visionary, susceptible to chance.</u>

J. K. Burnett, the son of Wesley Burnett, used the words "sometimes foolhardy," to describe his father; a father he respected and loved. A review of some of the incidents in Wesley's life, gives credence to this evaluation.

Wesley Burnett, against his better judgment, took off after marauding Indians, and almost got killed in the process. He drove his wagons with perilous abandon. He borrowed against debt-free property, to obtain new land. He continually exposed himself to danger, injury or loss. His life was one of jeopardy!

J.K. further reports, "My father was always a fast and rather reckless driver. There were no brakes on the wagons he drove. His horses knew well the necessity of keeping out of the way of the wagon when going downhill. Off they would gallop – horses, wagon and my father in a great cloud of dust. No effort was ever made to hold back. My father seemed to greatly enjoy this kind of driving,"

J. K. writes again, "One evening my father was crossing the railroad tracks with his team and wagon near Gilroy, California. While on the tracks, the approaching locomotive blew its whistle. All four horses stopped stone still and refused to budge. The train commenced to slow up and my father, always one to take a chance, gambled that the engine would stop before it hit the wagon. He stayed on his seat and won. But the nose of the cow-catcher was under the side of the wagon when the train finally stopped. I asked him why he did not leave the seat and jump to safety. His reply was, 'Ah, I was sure the engineer would stop the engine before it hit the wagon.'"

One night Wesley Burnett was coming back from San Luis Obispo to the Coast Ranch. He had a passenger by the name of Taylor. The darkness did not inhibit Wesley. He hit the Cayucos Creek at some speed, missing the wagon track. The wagon turned over in the mud, throwing Taylor out on his head. This left him unconscious for some time. Wesley was also thrown out. The wagon had rolled over him, pinning him under the load. Fortunately, the horses, although spirited, did not move. Eventually, Taylor gained consciousness, and called out to Wesley, "What can I do?" Wesley yelled, "Lift the wagon off of me!" Taylor, a strong man, was able to lift the heavy wagon just enough to free Wesley. He emerged muddy but unhurt. The two men were able to right and reload the wagon. They arrived back at the ranch shortly after midnight.

Apparently, Wesley Burnett did not change his ways. The December 13, 1893, edition of the San Luis Obispo Tribune reports:

A Prominent Citizen Meets With a Very Serious Accident

Mr. Wesley Burnett, a large land holder in this county, had a very narrow escape from having his neck broken Monday night. He left this city at 5 o'clock p.m. in his buggy with his intent of crossing over the grade. When about 200 yards past the first saloon on the grade, he met the stage on the way to the city. His horse became frightened at the noise and began to plunge so that Mr. Burnett could not handle him, and as a consequence man, horse and buggy went over the grade together. It was so dark that the accident was unnoticed by those on board the stage, which rolled by, leaving Mr. Burnett bruised and unconscious some forty feet below the grade. He must have been unconscious for about two hours. When consciousnesses returned he observed a man with a lantern some distance away to whom he called for assistance. His voice being very weak, the man could not locate him for some time.

Later he was taken with great difficulty to the saloon, from whence he was brought back to this city. His injuries were comparatively light, when compared to the distance he fell and the obstacles he struck. His chest is considerably bruised and he fears that he received some internal injury, as it is with great difficulty that he is able to breath.

One of the shaves of the buggy was run through the right fore-leg of the horse, which otherwise was not much hurt. The buggy was smashed into small pieces.

Wesley Burnett, at the age of 74, had taken off in his buggy, pulled by a spirited horse, for a run over a rough mountain pass, on a cold January night. He had expected to make a high speed twenty-one-mile ride from San Luis Obispo to Templeton, California. Courageous? Foolhardy? Most would judge, a bit of both!

Wesley Burnett's deadly encounters with the grizzly bears, when armed with only a single-shot muzzle-loaded rifle and his high-stakes involvement in land acquisition are previously recorded. Wesley Burnett was never one to take the easy road.

In the critical area of marriage, one sees a romantic and impulsive Wesley Burnett. Certainly his statement, "Boys, that's the woman I'm going to marry," when he first laid eyes on the beautiful Mary Kennedy, could logically be deemed "impulsive." Or, as it might seem in retrospect, directed by the Divine? Whichever it was, Wesley's ability to act decisively can be seen as a positive. He was a man of action!

However, this perceived quality did not serve him well in another significant relational decision. It is now I write with some trepidation. Here is the reason. In a hundred and forty-year period, no family record or family discussion ever revealed that Wesley Burnett, at the age of 74, and fourteen years after Mary's death, married Hilda Wengren, a Swedish girl, some forty years younger than he.

The recorded marriage certificate shows the union took place on September 31, 1892, in Templeton: a town six miles south of Paso Robles. Wesley and Hilda had one child – a boy named Willard. No date was ever recorded for his birth. It seems that Wesley and Hilda were separated. Hilda and her son Willard are shown in the city directories for San Jose, from 1901 to 1932. What actually happened to them remains shrouded in family mystery. At the time of Wesley's death, the obituary in the <u>Paso Robles Daily News</u> reported, "Wesley Burnett leaves five children, three daughters and two sons to mourn his death." No mention was ever made of his wife or his son, Willard. One might look at Wesley's decision to marry a woman forty years his junior as a bit "reckless," which assuredly brought pain to all involved.

This family incident is mentioned, not only to complete the record, but to use the negatives in life as positives for the generations to come. One studies history to understand the present. The hope is to mitigate in our own lives that which has proven to be destructive in others.

*   *   *

Wesley Burnett maintained his God-fearing faith and rugged independence throughout his adventurous and often difficult life. He, like others of his kind, toiled on the frontiers to establish California, a golden new empire on the shores of the Pacific. Let us remember with wonder and appreciation. Wesley Burnett was a man for the ages.

*   *   *

WESLEY BURNETT TOMBSTONE

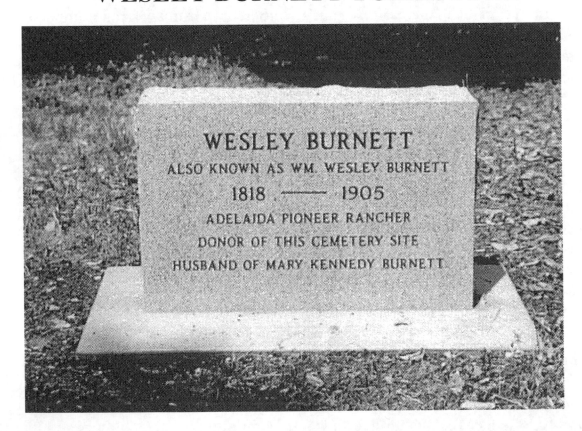

In later years, Wesley's grave was marked only by a small block of cement, unlettered and void of identification. Then in 2001, his great-granddaughter, Louise Holler Craddock, and her husband Sheldon, placed, at the Nacimiento Cemetery, an engraved headstone on the grave of Wesley Burnett.

WESLEY BURNETT
1818 – 1905

Picture Courtesy of Louise Holler Craddock

     This is an early photograph of Wesley Burnett (or possible a tin-type) taken about the time he settled above the Nacimiento River in northern San Louis Obispo County, 1860.

     Wesley Burnett lived out his years as a respected and prosperous rancher, maintaining a God-fearing, self-reliant independence throughout his adventurous, often difficult life. He, like others of his kind, toiled through the frontiers to establish California: a golden new empire on the shores of the Pacific.

ADELAIDA AREA of SAN LUIS OBISPO COUNTY
Hatched areas indicate property owned by
Wesley Burnett in 1883 California

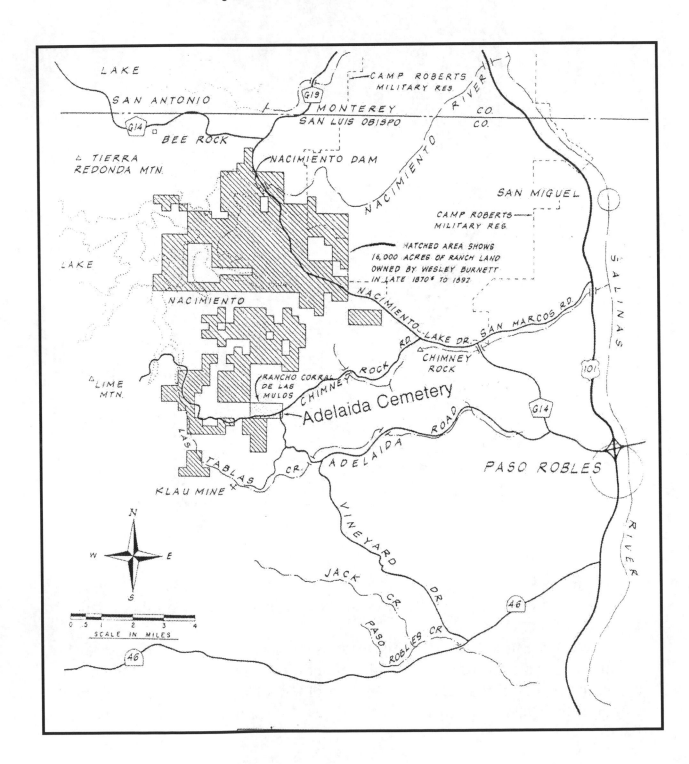

WESLEY BURNETT RANCH LANDS
1870 to 1892

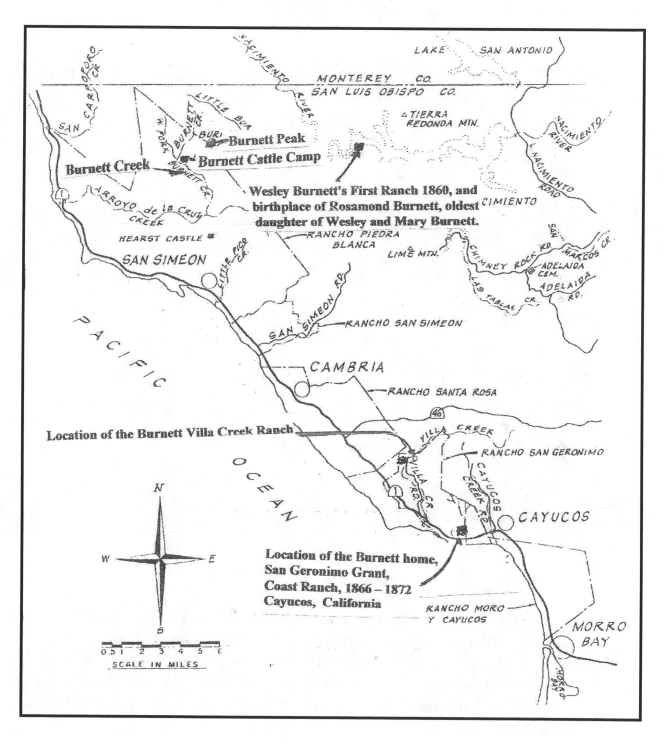

**Burnett landmarks in San Luis Obispo County
Including locations of his ranches**

HISTORIC PICTURE – BLACKSMITH SHOP
1867

Cayucos, California

The Blacksmith Shop at Cayucos, around the time of the Civil War until the turn of the century, was a focal point for the early farmers, sheep and cattlemen of the area. Here the horses were shod and the equipment repaired. Wesley Burnett, owner of the Coast Ranch, which was a part of the historic Geronimo grant, was a respected and regular customer.

ROSAMOND BURNETT ROBINSON
1863 – 1918

Rosamond Burnett Robinson, daughter of William Wesley Burnett and Mary Kennedy Burnett, was born in December 1863 on her parents homestead on the Nacimiento River in northern San Luis Obispo County. California. The log-cabin in which she was born was on the south side of the river, about four miles west of where the Las Tables joined the Nacimiento River. The cabin had a cobblestone fireplace used for cooking and heating. Near the house was a barn made of logs, and they drew water from a well her father had dug nearby. Their only neighbors were the James Lynch family, who lived five miles away on the opposite side of the river.

Several hundred cattle grazed on the land around their home and undoubtedly some of the first sounds this baby girl heard were the bawls of cattle in the night when attacked by the grizzly bears. There were bears around the ranch and her father killed many of them with his muzzle-loader to protect his herd. From the time she was a baby, the family always called her "Rosa," short for Rosamond.

When Rosa was one year old, the great California drought of 1864 hit the land. The country parched under day after day of blistering heat. Livestock all over the state died by the thousands. At the end of the year the family was left with a herd of less than a hundred cattle; a tremendous loss from the one thousand Wesley had only twelve months earlier. Her father knew there was more grass on the Pacific side of the San Luis Mountains, so in the fall of 1865, the family moved to the coastal section of the county. There they settled on what was supposed to be government land on Villa Creek.

Their sad experience while at Villa Creek is chronicled in the stories of her parents Wesley and Mary Burnett. Two events, while there, made a lasting impression on Rosa. One was the flood. The rushing water ravaged the ranch.

91

It carried off livestock, and raged for a night through the cabin. The other memory is of her mother being kicked and injured by a horse that balked; an injury from which Mary Burnett never fully recovered.

Rosa's fondest memories as a child were of the years her family spent on the Coast Ranch her father purchased from a Spaniard by the name of Jose Castros. This beautiful coastal land was originally a part of the historic San Geronimo Grant. On May 25, 1866, the transaction was completed, and in the weeks that followed the Burnett family moved to the new ranch.

They selected a building site approximately one and one-quarter miles north on the coast road from the present town of Cayucos. From there one turns right on Geronimo Grant, a dirt road that parallels a small creek. About two hundred yards up from the coast road, one will now find a number of small buildings. One old building along the southwest side of the creek, with a shed attached, is what remains of the original Burnett cabin. This is the home where Rosa grew up, built shortly after the Civil War. The original cabin had a dirt floor. In 1994, one would see an old wood floor in the cabin. This floor was constructed in later years. Regardless, this was the location of Rosa's home during her carefree and formative years.

Here are further directions which will help others locate the original Burnett home site. The creek by the house comes down what they called Big Canyon. This creek opens up into the heart of the Coast Ranch. A smaller creek drains Little Canyon, southwest of the house, and joins the larger creek near where the house was built. The cabin was built of pine lumber bought at a sawmill near the present town of Cambria. At first, it consisted of two rooms: the main part of the house was one room with no floor, and the second room was an attached shed. For the first two or three years, the family cooked in a stone fireplace.

Rosamond loved to play with her older brother, Bud, and her baby sister, Helen, in the lagoon across the coast road from their house. Many happy hours of Rosa's childhood were spent at the lagoon and along the shore, where the ocean splashed, filling depressions in the rock with sea water. There in the ocean, west of the creek and lagoon, was a jagged sea ridge she called Diamond Point. A few yards south of Diamond Point, near the bank of the ocean, was a large, rifted, flat rock area. Rosa discovered a number of large holes, about six-inches across. This was where the Indians had ground grain with their pestles, as they prepared their food. Rosa would sit there by the hour, contemplating her aloneness and the mysterious beauty around her.

In the ocean, off the shore from the lagoon, were two large rocks, which could be reached at low tide. The lower of the two rocks was flat and covered with mussels. The children named it Mussel Rock. The other rock was pointed, more like a tent, and had big cracks filled with abalone. She called it Abalone Rock and often watched her brother collect these morsels of the sea. Two or three acres of rich soil surrounded the area. This is where the family planted their garden. A short distance up the coast was Seal Bay, an estuary teeming with rock fish. Brother Bud always kept the family in fresh seafood.

Up the draw from their house was considerable land for farming. To this day it is producing lush crops. Here, pumpkin and squash were planted for hog feed. The wild oats were cut for hay. A stock corral was built of Cambria Pine, and a corral for the hay was also built. In this picturesque coastal setting, Rosamond Burnett spent the major portion of her childhood. There were no schools, but her mother, Mary Burnett, was a teacher, who assured an excellent education for her children. During this time, too, Mary Kennedy Burnett gave birth to her seventh child, a little girl, Lillie, on December 22, 1869. From that time on, Rosa, who was seven years old, took increasing responsibilities for the family. Her mother never fully recovered from the injury she had sustained four years earlier, when kicked by a horse.

Sometime between December 1869 and 1872, the Burnett family moved from the Coast Ranch back to Adelaida and the Rancho de los Mulos. We know this because Mary's last child, William Wesley Burnett, was born in Adelaida in 1872. One thing is clear, the 1870's became increasingly difficult years for Rosamond. She was only ten years old. Her father was often away, actively involved in land acquisition. Too, there was a new baby brother to care for.

Then, one day, word came. Her half-brother John Cooper had been murdered in the South Seas; a tragedy that shook the entire family. Rosa was hit by these emotional burdens at such an early age, and they intensified with the death of her forty-six year old mother in 1878. Rosa was only fourteen years old, the oldest girl of the five remaining children, when her mother was buried on the ridge overlooking the ranch.

Rosamond's father never lost faith in the future. He knew his children were to play important roles in the growing development of the State of California. This could not be done without their education. This meant college for all the children. At the age of seventeen, Rosamond was sent to Los Angeles, where the University of Southern California was being organized. There she met a young man from Kings County by the name of John Wesley Robinson. A romance developed. Rosamond Burnett, and her fiancé, John Wesley Robinson, received their diplomas in 1865. They were both members of the first class to graduate from the University of Southern California.

The following year, 1886, she married John Wesley Robinson, who had a productive farm in Grangeville, near Hanford, California. It was in Grangeville where her first two sons were born. The oldest was Burnett Robinson, 1887, and next was Franklin Willard Robinson, born May 27, 1889.

In 1890 they sold their ranch and moved to Los Angeles, so John could train for the ministry. These were difficult times again for Rosamond. She was lonely while her husband was back at U.S.C. preparing for the Methodist ministry. Then she was alone again while he traveled the state on Christian crusades. Worst of all, was being alone when her oldest son, Burnett, died suddenly of spinal meningitis. Some of the details of these years plagued by loneliness are recounted by my father, Franklin W. Robinson, in the story of his life.

After Burnett's death, the family made several moves to new pastorates. These included Guerneville, St. Helena, Ukiah and Fairfield. In 1904 they moved to Long Beach, California. There Rosamond lived out her years, many of them alone, as her husband traveled in his evangelistic work. Reminiscing many years later, her son Franklin said:

Mother was a very unusual character. She was a very spiritual woman. She believed in the power of prayer and thought anything could be accomplished through prayer. When my father was out holding his religious meetings, I can remember how my mother would go into sessions of prayer for their success. And then all of a sudden she would get release. She just knew these meetings were going to be a great success. Then in a few days we would get a letter from my father saying, the Spirit had fallen on the people, that they had had great results. Many came to the Lord.

Mother lived in a state of terrific poverty. Whenever tax or interest time came around, in order to meet these financial obligations, she would go into a session of prayer. In some way her prayers were always answered. Money would turn up to meet her obligations. We never starved, but we did live a very simple life. Mother knew she could pray herself out of any situation. She was something of a mystical person, clairvoyant I think you would call her. I can remember one time when her sister, Helen Borton, was in Mexico City. Her husband, Dr. Borton, was teaching in a school down there. Their daughter, Margaret, was living with them, and what a beautiful girl she was. Then one day Mother announced, "Something has happened to Margaret. I had a clear vision and saw Margaret dead, and in a casket." It was so real to Mother. She knew it was true. A few days later word arrived that after a brief and unknown illness, Margaret had died. Mother, without any question, had an extra-sensory perception. Any number of times she foresaw things that were going to happen. Along with this was her great spiritual faith in Christ, that through Him there were special powers released within us that transcended the physical realities of life.

Although Rosamond lived in faith, it is apparent that the burdens of poverty, tragedy, poor health and loneliness took their toll. In November 1911, she wrote the following to her son, Franklin, who was then a student at Columbia University in New York City,

I have had a partial nervous breakdown. The distress in my head was taken away in answer to prayer. My head was very bad. There were times when I couldn't talk to anyone, and my eyes felt as though something was drawing them back into my head. I was in a serious condition; my nerves are not very strong, but Faith is the victory. Read the wonderful chapter on Faith in Hebrews 11.

My father, Franklin Robinson, explained that the medical profession today would probably describe his mother's condition as acute depression. Franklin was filled with a deep sadness that his loving and committed mother experienced such pain and distress. The trying conditions under which Rosamond lived can be illustrated by recounting a portion of a letter to her son Franklin.

I don't know what Papa is going to do next year. He has been preaching this past year in San Miguel. They paid him the $900 they owed him for the year, but he wrote me that it would take it all to pay his debts. I expected him to have at least a hundred dollars over to help Mary with her college expenses. He has only sent home one hundred dollars this year, and paid fifty dollars interest on this sand lot here on the beach. As far as money goes, I can't count on him for much if any help to have sufficient income to get along. And too, it is so discouraging to be sick when I am so anxious to be well. But, I shall try to be patient in tribulation, rejoicing in hope and constant prayer.

At the beginning of the summer of 1913, her daughter, Mary, returned from Pomona College. This beautiful and brilliant girl had been in deteriorating health throughout the spring semester. On July 30, she died of tuberculosis. Her mother, Rosamond Burnett Robinson, shortly after her daughter's death, wrote the following:

Rosemary's Message

The Lord planted a sweet flower in our home, to bloom for twenty-two beautiful years—then He came and picked that pure sweet flower and planted it in His home above, to bloom there forever. My treasure is in Heaven. "Where your treasure is there will your heart be also." (Matthew 6:21) Heaven seems very near, now that Mary has gone home.

In the early morning of July 30th, the angels came and took her so sweetly and quietly away that ere we knew it she was gone. We did not think she was going to leave us. We expected her to get well. I felt I could not give her up until I knew the will of the Lord. I went into the next room, and shut myself up with Jesus. I asked Him to let me know his will at this time. This is the hour in every one's life when Jesus is the only one who can speak peace to the troubled heart.

I was waiting alone with Jesus when a voice said, "Be still and know I am God. Take the shoes from your feet, for this is Holy ground." Again, I heard the voice, which said, "Look! Look! Look! Then I saw Mary's sweet face smiling at me, and Jesus was standing by her side.

Then I saw a path going up a rugged mountain. I could see Rosemary in a beautiful place on the top of the mountain, where it was all sunlight. Flowers were blooming everywhere. She picked a pure white lily, and was waving it in her hand. Mary's face was radiant with joy. There were countless others there. She called out to me, "Oh Mama, Mama, come up here Mama. I'm so happy and free. This is a beautiful place up here, come up here Mama. Oh Mama, I'm so happy and free. This is a beautiful place. Come on Mama. Tell Papa to come on. Tell Frank and John to come on; tell them to hurry up where I am. Tell my friends to come, Mama, Tell all my friends to come on. You'll tell them, won't you, Mama?"

She kept asking me this, and would not be satisfied until I said, "Yes, Mary, yes dear, I'll tell them all to come."

Then Mary waved her hand and said, "Good-bye, Mama, good-bye for a little while. Tell all my friends good-bye for a little while,"

Dear friend, I cannot convey to you in words the great comfort and peace, which this brought to our sorrowing hearts. I could not grieve after seeing Rosemary so happy and safe with Jesus. I love Jesus as never before, and my heart is filled with gratitude to Him, that he would permit me to see Rosemary, and let her speak with me. Now I have this message to give Mary's loved ones and friends.

I have given Rosemary's message to you word for word, as nearly as possible, and I trust you will receive it as a message direct from Heaven to you, that even in her death, she may win souls for Jesus. I am sending her message out to all her friends to fulfill the sacred promise she made me give her. "Yes dear, I'll tell them all to come."

"Eye hath not seen, nor ear heard, neither have entered into the heart of man the things which God hath prepared for them that love Him."

I Corinthians 2:9

Rosemary's Mother, Rosamond Burnett Robinson

*   *   *

Four years later Rosamond, too, was taken in death. Her son Franklin remembers:

My mother was in very poor health during those last years. I don't remember exactly what her difficulty was, but I remember very well, after a physical examination, the doctor told her she had an enlarged spleen. This might have caused her trouble, but I have never really heard of such a thing. At any rate, she died very suddenly in her little bungalow home. She lived between Ninth and Tenth Streets, on Locust Avenue in Long Beach. That was 1918. Unfortunately, she never got to see her first grand child: Franklin Willard Robinson Junior. Willard was born a couple of months after her death.

Mother was always in favor of the ministry to which father devoted his life. It did make for a very difficult time for her. Alone, she carried the responsibility to raise and care for the family. She lived out her life with a quiet and unusual courage. This needs to be known by the following generations!

Her advice, written to her oldest son Franklin in 1911, can touch us all:

Walk very softly before the Lord. Lift up your heart to Him in thankfulness and praise. Read your Bible daily, and pray without ceasing. Be of the world, but unspotted from it.

Mama

Rosamond Burnett Robinson was buried in the family plot, next to her beloved children, Burnett and Mary, at the Evergreen Cemetery in Los Angeles.

GENEALOGY OF ROSA BURNETT (ROBINSON)

**Rosamond Burnett (Robinson)
b. 1863, Nacimiento, CA
m. 1886, Parkfield, CA
d. May 2, 1978, Long Beach, CA**

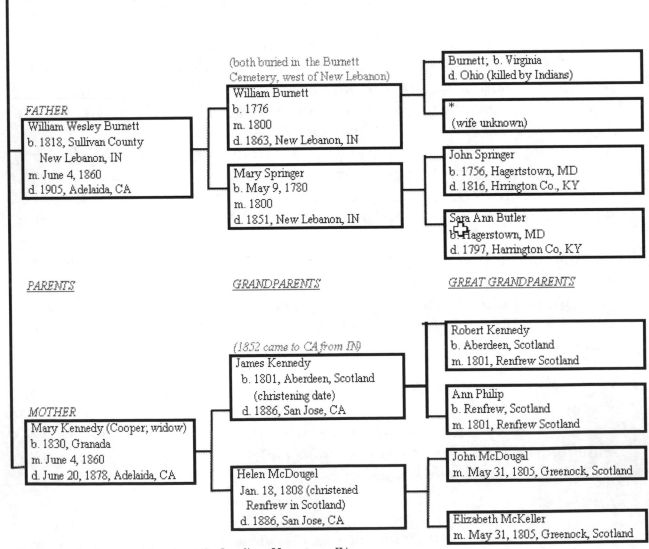

(both buried in the Burnett
Cemetery, west of New Lebanon)

FATHER

William Wesley Burnett
b. 1818, Sullivan County
    New Lebanon, IN
m. June 4, 1860
d. 1905, Adelaida, CA

William Burnett
b. 1776
m. 1800
d. 1863, New Lebanon, IN

Mary Springer
b. May 9, 1780
m. 1800
d. 1851, New Lebanon, IN

Burnett; b. Virginia
d. Ohio (killed by Indians)

*
    (wife unknown)

John Springer
b. 1756, Hagertstown, MD
d. 1816, Hrrington Co., KY

Sara Ann Butler
b. Hagerstown, MD
d. 1797, Harrington Co, KY

PARENTS   *GRANDPARENTS*   *GREAT GRANDPARENTS*

(1852 came to CA from IN)

James Kennedy
 b. 1801, Aberdeen, Scotland
    (christening date)
 d. 1886, San Jose, CA

Robert Kennedy
b. Aberdeen, Scotland
m. 1801, Renfrew Scotland

Ann Philip
b. Renfrew, Scotland
m. 1801, Renfrew Scotland

MOTHER

Mary Kennedy (Cooper; widow)
b. 1830, Granada
m. June 4, 1860
d. June 20, 1878, Adelaida, CA

Helen McDougel
Jan. 18, 1808 (christened
    Renfrew in Scotland)
d. 1886, San Jose, CA

John McDougal
m. May 31, 1805, Greenock, Scotland

Elizabeth McKeller
m. May 31, 1805, Greenock, Scotland

* The Burnett family came to America at the founding of Jamestown, VA
  and claimed relationship to Thomas Burnett Bishop of Canterbury.

ROCK BLUFFS OF THE
BURNETT COAST RANCH
Cayucos, California

Willard Robinson, grandson of Rosa Robinson Burnett,
looks over a portion of the three-mile coastline
of the Burnett ranch.

Joan Robinson inspects the
Indian mortars, where the
Burnett children played in the late
1860's in
Cayucos, California

ROSAMOND BURNETT ROBINSON
1863 - 1918

My mother lived her life with a quiet and unusual courage.
Her advice was to walk softly before the Lord.
Lift up your heart to Him in thankfulness and praise.
Be of the world, but unspotted from it.

Franklin Robinson, 1975

THE WESLEY BURNETT HOME
Built in 1866

Coast Ranch, Cayucos, California

"Father and Mother selected the building site for our new home at the Coast Ranch near Cayucos. They chose a place on Big Creek. It was in the valley, a short distance above the wagon road, which went along the coast from Cayucos to Cambria. California.   Father had the lumber milled in Cambria, and hauled it the thirty-mile round tip with the team and wagon. The one-room cabin had a dirt floor, and Mother cooked in the fireplace. Later, we built a shed on one side of the cabin."

Rosa Burnett Robinson

The deteriorating cabin, built during the Civil War, still stands in 2007. This is a hundred and twenty-two years after it was built.

NOTE REGARDING CAUSE OF DEATH FOR ROSAMUND BURNETT ROBINSON

In January, 2008, my cousin, Louise Craddock, sent a copy of my grandmother's death certificate. She had discovered it in her genealogy files under the "Medical Certificate of Death." It states:

> *The cause of death was as follows:*
> *Valvular disease of the heart.*

Thus, after ninety years of family confusion over the cause of death, the true cause has been established.

FRANKLIN WILLARD ROBINSON
1889-1978

I begin this re-write of my father's story almost thirty years after his death in Long Beach, California at the age of eighty-nine years. As I look back, I realize how often his remarkable life set goals for those of us who follow. Also, many of his traits were reflections not only of his parents, but those I discovered in the Kennedy and Burnett lines of his ancestral heritage. His personal story is the logical crown for this family history. As much of his story as possible will be recounted in his own words. Shortly before his death, I had my father record his memories on tape. This I have interspersed with my own recollections, where it appears appropriate. He began:

Well, this is quite a story. If I went into detail I would have to cover a lot of early California History. All of my grandparents came to California in covered wagons in the 1850s. In fact, my father was only four years old when he came with his parents. Although my mother was born in San Luis Obispo County in 1863, both of her parents, before her marriage, had crossed the plains by ox team. My grandfather Burnett came in the spring of 1850 in the early days of the gold rush. His cousin was Peter Burnett, who was the first governor of California. He had come over the Oregon Trail and later made his way by horseback south from Oregon to California.

My parents met while attending college at the University of Southern California. They were in the first graduating class. Following graduation, they returned to my father's ranch at a little place called Grangeville in Kings County. It is not too far from Hanford in the San Joaquin Valley. I was born on their ranch, May 27, 1889.

Soon after I was born, Father was offered a hundred-thousand dollars for his ranch. That was a lot of money in those days, and cleared the way for him to go back to the University of Southern California for study to become a Methodist minister. Father felt he had a real call. There was fire in his voice, he loved the Lord, and he knew he had the qualities needed in evangelistic work. We took off for Los Angeles so Father could prepare for the Christian ministry.

He bought a home on Pasadena Avenue in Los Angeles. It was located just before reaching the Highland Park area on the way from Los Angeles to Pasadena.

Father became an evangelist. His brother Frank Robinson, who was a great singer, would travel up and down the state holding revival meetings. Mother, Burnett my older brother, my sister, Mary and I would stay at home on the three acre plot on Pasadena Avenue. In my memory, it was like a ranch. When I saw it again in later years it seemed so much smaller. As a young boy, I remember running down to the bluff overlooking the railroad tracks. I loved to sit on a post and wave at the engineer as the trains rolled past.

We got around by horse and buggy. My father always kept a good horse, but we didn't travel throughout the state by horse. We took the Southern Pacific train up and down the coast from San Francisco to Los Angeles. We could do this because the railroad tracks had just been completed over the San Luis Mountains between Paso Robles and San Luis Obispo. That was quite a ride. One of the longest parts of the trip was through the San Fernando Valley—an endless stretch of nothing but desert and grain fields. Now it is all one endless city.

I remember seeing the first automobile that came into Los Angeles. It was a very big lumbering, touring machine with giant wheels that came down Pasadena Avenue. They let all the kids out of school. We were about two blocks away and we began running when we heard it coming. Smoke poured out of the tail end of the thing. It was an old chug-chug affair with three or four people in it. Now very few people remember the first automobile to hit Los Angeles, but that's a vivid memory for me. I was seven years old and I chased that old car until it went out of sight.

When I was eight years old, Burnett, who was eleven years old and such strength to my mother, was knocked down by fever. He had spinal meningitis and was gone in a few days. I remember it very well—very vividly. I was so frightened. The doctor came and tried to treat him—put him in ice tubs---anything to control his fever. But he died and it was a very sad time for our family. My father did not get home until after Burnett was gone. He said he did not want to leave the family again, and decided to seek a pastorate and give up his traveling evangelistic work.

I was in second grade when Father was appointed to his first pastorate. It was a little town on the Russian River north of San Francisco called Guerneville. In those days a Methodist minister never stayed over two years in any one place. So, after a year or two in Guerneville we went to St. Helena. I rang the bell in the steeple every Sunday morning to call the people to worship. From St. Helena we moved to Ukiah, and from Ukiah to Fairfield. This was interesting because this was the little town west of Sacramento where my father had arrived as a four year old boy with his parents after their long trip from St. Joseph, Missouri to California by ox-team in1859. Fairfield was where I finished my grammar school education in 1903.

By this time my father decided that he wanted to take his family to an area that would provide some more advantages. Also, he was restless! He couldn't get over the desire to resume his evangelistic work. To do this he needed a permanent location for his family while he pursued his preaching circuit. He had always dreamed of Long Beach, California as being just the right place. I had heard quite a bit about Long Beach, and I remembered the good times we had there when we went to the beach for Methodist picnics back during the time we lived in Los Angeles. In those days Long Beach was a little village, "a silver strand by a sapphire sea," where they held Methodist camp meetings.

Well, we did move there. That was in 1904. Long Beach has been my home ever since. I went to Polytechnic High School when the population of Long Beach was 2,500. We had a great debate team. It was more important than football in those days and it was a real honor when I was elected captain of the debate team.

This ends the reminiscences of my father's early years as he told them. I was interested in a letter I found many years later. It had been written by his younger brother, John Robinson in April, 1912. It verifies my father's success as a high school debater, a talent that later opened the opportunity for him to gain a college education. It read:

Dear Frank,

Poly High School has won a number of pennants since you were here, but none in debating. The only debating pennant in our large and beautiful school collection is the one you won for Long Beach High. It hangs on the auditorium wall in a conspicuous place. In our rallies they all tell about the old victorious times in debating when you were here. In a recent assembly they told about the great spirit they had in the days of Robinson--how they won those great victories for the school and how the students supported the

105

team, rain or shine. Your name is often used to stir up school spirit.   Now don't get all puffed up.

Good-bye from your loving brother,   *John W. Robinson*

The fact that the family was often in a state of poverty was accepted by Franklin in those early days. Later the memory of those difficult years provided a tremendous drive in him to provide financial security for his own family. Whenever tax or interest time came around, his mother would go into a session of prayer. It was up to her to meet these obligations, because his father was gone, preaching up and down the state on his evangelistic circuit. "Money", my father said, "would always turn up to meet these obligations. We never starved. We lived very simply."

Franklin Robinson did have an outstanding school record and became prominent in speech and debate. This earned him a scholarship to the University of Southern California in 1908.   He continued his scholastic and forensic achievement at USC for the first two years of his college experience: 1909 and 1910. During the spring of 1910 he entered a public speaking contest that would change the course of his life. Speaking on the subject, "America's New Awakening," he won the right to represent the University of Southern California in the Western States finals in Oregon. Whoever could win this tournament would go on to the national championships in Valparaiso, Indiana. He saw this as the challenge of his young life. On May, 25, 1910, just two days before his twentieth birthday, he left for the great adventure.   He recalls the event:

Today I made my final preparations for the trip. I washed my clothes in the morning, packed them in my suitcase and took it downtown to the train. I spent two hours working on my speech with the pastor of the First Methodist Church, because he was a great orator. I met my mother at noon and told her I had bought a ticket that would take me clear to Boston, as I just knew I must go to the East, whether I won the contest or not. She told me good-bye. I put the finishing touches on my delivery, as I stood on the back of the moving observation car.

The next day my father got on the train at San Luis Obispo and went with me as far as San Miguel, where he was preaching. He said, "You can do it!" He wished me well. We shook hands and said good-bye. I was in San Francisco for my 20th birthday. Uncle Wesley Burnett and Aunt Viola were there to meet me. Uncle Wesley gave me a $20 dollar gold piece and Aunt

Viola fitted me out with gloves, a new shirt with white collars and a necktie . I was ready for the contest.

I relate the details of the public speaking contest, for I believe it gives great insight into the way he approached and analyzed the many endeavors of his life. On May 30, 1910, Franklin Robinson took the train from Portland to McMinnville, Oregon , where the western oratorical finals were to be held. One of the students from the college met the train and took him to the campus. My father remembers:

Those I met impressed me as narrow but good-hearted fellows from the country. I was taken up to a little room in an old fashioned rambling house with no modern conveniences. It was a hot afternoon. I took a nap for two hours and then had a cold shower. My nerves were calm as I walked slowly down to the theater where the contest was held at 8 o'clock in the evening, I looked over the contestants and considered Tolleson of the University if Washington my strongest opponent. We all sat on the platform. The theater was filled with students and town people. They were very enthusiastic in their support for the Oregon representative. He had a well-written, fiery speech, but was very awkward in his delivery. He was six-foot two-inches tall, thin, light haired and had a boyish face and a high pitched voice. He put considerable force into his speech, but his gestures were very mechanical. He was rather a conceited fellow and was confident of winning. He took his defeat very hard.

Tolleson of Washington followed with a speech clearly stating the evils of the liquor traffic and radically defending the Prohibition Party as the solution to the problem. He was a developed speaker. His well proportioned body, strong face, clear voice, becoming gestures and easy manner gave him the attention of the house. He was twenty-seven years old and the winner of several contests in Washington.

Kruger of the University of California at Berkeley spoke next. He had been married a few days before and brought his wife to the contest. The prospect of an Eastern honeymoon trip caused him to put forth his best efforts to gain first honors. He was rather short with light curly hair. His pipe was a constant companion and the beer jug an acquaintance. His speech was well-named: "The Traitor within the State." His speech was delivered well. His voice was deep and resonant, but the tense muscles in his arms caused his gestures to appear stiff.

When the three judges, all strong defenders of the Prohibition cause, went to work on selecting the winners, the symphony orchestra played. Their rendition was interesting at first, but then it got rather monotonous. We had a long wait before they awarded the prizes. When the decision was made, the head judge came forward. He kept us in suspense for some time with his dry wit before he finally, with a broad smile on his face and words of pleasure, called Mr. Kruger of the University of California forward. We all thought he had been awarded the first prize. Mrs. Kruger was joyful as her husband went to the platform with a happy look. But that all faded when he returned from the platform with dejected spirits after being announced as the second place winner.

After further delay, he called me forth as the first prize winner. I was rather unstrung by the contest and the long wait afterwards, so I tossed about in my bed that night until about three or four in the morning.

*   *   *

The next day, June 12, 1910, the young Franklin took the northern train route through Seattle and the Canadian Rockies on his way to the national championships to be held in Valparaiso, Indiana. He wrote, "I took the train to the heart of the Rockies at Glacier. The snow and the ice came down to the track. The rugged peaks behind, the waterfalls and the rivers rushing through the gorges made it the most fantastic sight I had ever seen." Franklin Robinson went on to win the National Oratorical Contest. Letters and telegrams came in. A hometown boy from the far west coast brought Long Beach and the University of Southern California national recognition!

He went on to New York and enrolled at Columbia University in the fall of 1910, with $18.00 in his hand. A hundred-and-seventy-five-dollar scholarship, with which he had been awarded, was a great help, but that went for tuition. The two and a half years he spent at Columbia were exciting, growing, challenging and a confusing period in his life. He entered into the college community with the same zeal and drive that characterized his entire life. But the beckoning successes of the materialistic world came in conflict with the deep spiritual roots of his heritage. He never fully resolved this conflict.

Soon, the young Franklin became the editor of the <u>Columbia Spectator</u>, one of the outstanding university newspapers in the United States. In fact, it was the first daily college newspaper in America. He was also elected president of the Alpha Chi Rho fraternity. He immediately laid out his plan for success.

"Brothers", he said, "this is a critical year for Alpha Chi Rho and every precaution must be taken to ensure our success. This is the plan:

Shape up!
1. We need the proper appearance of the house.
2. Our finances are to be accountable and firmed up.
3. The Steward's department is to be reorganized.
4. It is our responsibility to bring in a strong "rush class."

Franklin Robinson's administrative qualities were readily accepted by his colleagues, but how to direct these talents would be a life-long challenge for him. He was a person of multiple gifts. His mother wrote

You are a child of many prayers. Recognize His leading and walk humbly. Be a man of faith and prayer.

She always wanted him to employ his gifts in dynamic ministry and preaching, a thought Franklin rejected throughout his life, often with a sense of guilt. This did plague him throughout the years.

Then, there was a poignant letter from his beloved sister, which confirmed his sense of political mission for his life:

Frank, I think God has chosen you to solve a great problem for our country. I wonder sometimes if you ever have that feeling? Lincoln got that feeling and he put an end to slavery, which was the problem of the 18th century. I really believe that!

With love (lots), Mary Rose Robinson

His college years, too, became a time of introspection for Franklin. Law had an increasing fascination for him. A legal background would open the door to a number of possibilities for a professional life. He wrote his esteemed uncle, W.W. Burnett in 1911, discussing the possibility of a career in law with him. By this time he had made up his mind to earn his law degree at Columbia University. His uncle replied:

Dear Frank,
Your letter was received and I am pleased to learn of your studies in law. If you could join me, we sure could make a go of it. When you get ready, come on out. I have two large suites that now house three attorneys. Take your time, get ready and we can do business.
Affectionately, your Uncle W. W. Burnett, San Francisco, California

Two other letters received by Franklin during the year of 1911 became prophetic in determining the future course of his life. Both of these letters were from his father. Here are parts of the correspondence:

Long Beach is growing fast and is a beautiful city. This is going to make my sand lot on the bluff overlooking the ocean very valuable. I could build an apartment house that would cost $150,000. That would bring in $900 per month. I figure twenty-four apartments at $40.00 each. If you will finance the building by getting a loan from those New York Bankers at 4%, I will join you as a partner.

And then, on June 5, 1911, this letter in which he heard for the first time the name of the young lady who someday would become his wife. His father wrote:

Your sister, Mary, is going up to Parkfield on the seventeenth to join the Brother Gould family on a wagon trip to Yosemite. Their daughter Hope graduates from high school this month and they wanted the girls to meet and share this wagon camping experience.

Well, take an old man's advice. Keep your record clean! I am thoroughly convinced that it makes no difference how much a man knows, or how big a home he can swing, if he is not clean, he is a dismal failure. Much love, I am your affectionate father, J.W. Robinson

*   *   *

Franklin worked during the summers tutoring boys from wealthy New York families in their studies and escorting them on their vacations. This took him one summer to a beautiful estate in Seal Harbor, Maine. These tutoring jobs provided him with the needed money to pay his rent at 633 W. 115th Street in New York, and his school expenses until he graduated with a degree in law from Columbia University in 1912.

His first job, after returning home to southern California, was as a furniture salesman in Los Angeles. This gave him needed financial support, while developing contacts necessary before building an apartment hotel on the Long Beach property with his father.

During this time Mary Robinson continued to encourage him to meet Anna Hope Gould, who had become her good friend on the wagon trip to Yosemite. But, Franklin was not interested in making the long trip to Parkfield in Monterey County. Mary's health continued to deteriorate, while she was a student at Pomona College. In the early morning of July 30, 1913 this beautiful and brilliant girl of twenty-two quietly died of tuberculosis. Again, deep tragedy had touched the family. The loss of his loving sister deeply affected Franklin. He became introspective. Later he told me:

I guess the loss of Mary made me start thinking again about Hope and how much she meant to my sister. I had a need to meet this girl who had meant so much to Mary. Anna Hope was spending her summers between her school years at College of Pacific, then in San Jose, and her parents' stock-farm at Parkfield, some thirty miles east of Paso Robles.

I took the train to my uncle's ranch on the Nacimiento River, in southern Monterey County. He loaned me his 1912 Oakland automobile to make the trip over to Parkfield, I made quite an impression as I drove into the valley. It was such a rare sight to see an automobile in those days. When a farmer saw me coming, he would get on the party-line and warn his neighbors that an automobile was on the way and to get their horses off the road so they wouldn't bolt.

I got to the ranch by the middle of the afternoon. Mr. Gould heard the car coming and he came out to the gate to greet me. He took me to meet his daughter who was in the summer kitchen doing dishes. Hope was embarrassed to be found in her kitchen apron! That was the beginning of the romance that eventually established our family. It didn't take me long to realize that Hope Gould was a very special person.

Franklin Robinson married Hope Gould on October 31, 1916, at the Gould family home on the ranch at Parkfield, California. Here is his recollection of that important day:

It started early. Dad Gould went with me. We left Parkfield in my old touring automobile and drove over the mountains to Paso Robles. There we took the train to Salinas. That's where we had to go to get the marriage license. Father had taken the train in from San Francisco, where he had been on a preaching mission. We met in Salinas, so we could ride back to Paso Robles together. It all clicked and we got back to the ranch in time for a big family dinner Mother Gould had prepared. Only a few of our closest friends were present. After dinner we stood up in the living room and Father tied the knot.

After the ceremony Hope, Father and I drove back to San Miguel where Father caught a train back to San Francisco. Hope and I then took the short drive south to Paso Robles where Hope and I spent our first night in the old Paso Robles Inn. It was quite a day.

Their first home was in a little bungalow in eastern Los Angeles. Franklin had a temporary job as a furniture salesman, just long enough to get a little money together to get ahead in Long Beach. He wanted to push ahead with the project of building a luxury apartment hotel. Shortly after arriving ln Long Beach, his mother suddenly and unexpectedly died. He had lost the third member of his family.

Shortly after, Franklin W. Robinson was launched on a business and civic career that established him as a respected leader in the booming community. The opening of the Sutherland (the original name of the Robinson Hotel) was a gala event in the history of Long Beach. He was an active member of Kiwanis and Vice President of the Chamber of Commerce. He joined the Virginia Country Club, where later he became President and began his life interest in social and competitive golf. Franklin's life was going well.

*   *   *

The Corona del Valle Ranch in the foothills of the western end of the Antelope Valley has been an important factor in the history of the Robinson family. Five generations of our family have lived, one time or another, on this unique and beautiful mountain ranch. Franklin Robinson recounts the series of unusual circumstances that came to pass in his initial purchase of the property:

The first time I ever saw the ranch was on the thirty-first day of October, 1917. Harold Sandberg had homesteaded the area. I had known about Mr. Sandburg and the ranch, because he had married a nurse who many years before had been in my Uncle Holler's home, when the family lived in Indiana. Her name was Mary and she came to the Antelope Valley for her health. It was there in the Antelope Valley she met Sandberg, was married, and became Mary Sandberg. Soon after she invited my Holler cousins, who had moved from Indiana to Hollywood, to come up to the Sandberg ranch for a visit.

The Holler family came back from their visit and told me, "That's the most beautiful place we have ever seen!" My cousin Wesley talked about the deer, the rabbits, the wild pigeons, the quail, and the view across the west end of the Antelope Valley to the Tehachapi Mountains, and the tremendous oak trees on the ranch. I so wanted to go up and see the place! So, on out first wedding anniversary I told Hope. "I would like to go up and see that old homestead ranch."

Sandburg had also built a lodge where we could stay at the summit of the Old Ridge Route, a real snake-grade up over the mountains between Los Angeles and Bakersfield. We decided to take a round trip in our 1915 Buick, through Palmdale, then west out of the valley on a dirt road to where Highway 138 now connects with the Old Ridge Route. We drove up the mountain to the Sandberg Lodge and stayed there in a comfortable little cabin. The next morning we woke to one of those beautiful October days. The air was pure. We could see for miles. After breakfast, Mr Sandberg invited us to go with him to the old ranch, which was three miles to the east, to get the milk, vegetables and fruit needed to supply the lodge. We piled into his spring-wagon and took off down-grade, and then through his apple orchard. From there the wagon road went by a giant oak grove, then over a hill on a winding dirt road to the ranch. There, between two of the largest oak trees I have ever seen, was his little farm cottage I had heard about. We sat on the porch and right then and there we made up our mind; someday we would own this ranch. It was one of those beautiful clear sharp fall days. How spectacular it was! I asked Mr. Sandberg how much he wanted for the ranch. He gave me a price of $14,000. He said there was a $10,000 mortgage on the property and it would take $4,000 to handle it. "Well, I don't have $4,000," I said. But I assured him that someday I would have the money.

Soon things would break for me. We began to get good income from the hotel we had built on the ocean front. We had enough money now to buy a view lot on Signal Hill. We soon built a Santa Fe type home with a beautiful view of Long Beach, the Pacific Ocean, and on clear days, Catalina Island. It was spectacular.

No sooner had we moved in, than the Shell Oil Company drilled an oil well just across Cherry Avenue from our new home. All of sudden there was a roar. It was a "gusher!" Oil shot up and sprayed black oil all over our new home. Then the gusher caught on fire! You could see it all over Long Beach. A picture of the well on fire was spread full-page over the January 1, 1922, Sunday edition of the Los Angeles Times. What a mess! This ended our living on Signal Hill. We tore town the house and drilled seven wells on the property. The Signal Hill oil field proved to be the richest oil field, per acre, in the world. Equally amazing is that Robinson #1, the first of the eight wells we drilled, proved to be the most productive well on Signal Hill. We found out later we had hit right on the northwest side of the Cherry Hill fault. The oil kept working its way up to the high point of the formation structure. Imagine! We had drilled in just the right spot. Many years later, the drilling companies went into secondary recovery for oil. This is when they flood the entire oil structure with water. Owners were then to be equally reimbursed for each well they owned. This really wasn't fair. Each owner should be reimbursed according to the percentage of oil each well had produced. I knew I had a good legal case against Texaco, but it took me a long time to get the dispute settled. Finally, Texaco did agree on paying us on the percentage basis that each of our wells had produced over the years. So, in the end, the family made out very well.

Here is an interesting fact. There is still a deep oil structure known as the brown zone that has never been tapped. It could realistically produce more oil than has been pumped out of Signal Hill in the last sixty years. Some day when the price of oil goes high enough, it will become economically feasible to drill into this vast pool of untapped oil. That's why the family should never sell their Signal Hill oil rights! But that's another matter.

With the oil money flowing in from our wells and the hotel, we had the prospect of a substantial income. Dad Gould and I went up to see Sandberg with the idea of closing a deal for the ranch. When we got there Mr Sandberg said we were too late—he had just closed a deal with a Mr. Danzinger who was a rich oil man from Westwood,. That sure let me down, but Sandburg suggested we drive over to the ranch the next morning to see what was going on. That was the disappointment of my life. Such activity! There must have been a hundred Mexicans camped there, all on the work crew. They were making adobe blocks to construct the big house and the bunk house. The Mexicans were building the forms to make the large adobe blocks, mixing the mud and setting the blocks in place. Whole crews were busy with teams of horses, clearing the land and preparing it for the planting of the orchards. Dad Gould shook his head and said. "You let something pretty good slip through your hands."

I found out later that Dansinger, the new owner, was nothing but a cheap promoter. He had married the wealthy Daisy Canfield and spent $100,000 of her money that first year in making this ranch one of the great show places in Los Angeles County. They called it Rancho Corona del Valle. This ranch certainly was to the true "crown of the valley". We returned to Long Beach. I was sick. My dream of owning this beautiful property would forever be beyond my reach.

A year passed. Then one day I got a call in Long Beach from a real-estate man by the name of Ruess. He told me that he had put together the original deal for Rancho Corona del Valle with Dansinger, and he knew I had been interested in the property. "The time is right for you to make an offer on the place," Ruess said.

"That's ridiculous." I told him. "I have no business taking on a place like that. I don't have that kind of money.

"Don't be so sure," Ruess said. He explained that after the first year, this fellow Dansinger had thrown a big party at the ranch with his friends. There was scandal over some Hollywood girls that had been imported, and Dansiger's wife found out. She was the one who had the money, was filing for divorce, and wanted to dump the ranch.

I did take Dad Gould back up there, though. We spent a night in the big house. It was all furnished with this beautiful furniture from Mexico City and the Mission Inn in Riverside, California. Colorful Navajo rugs covered the tile floors. There were thirteen barrels of wine in a hidden cellar. This was quite a risky thing in those days of prohibition. Ruess said for me to make an offer of $50,000 for everything—cattle, hogs, furniture, farm equipment, everything.

Well, I didn't want to go into debt for that much. My bankers came up and took a look at the place and thought I could handle a thirty thousand dollar deal. They would back me for that much. To make a long story short, the deal was put together. I soon owned the ranch.

It was perfect timing because the oil wells started coming in at full force and I began spending a lot of the money to further develop the ranch. We built a big hay barn, developed the Horse-Camp and the upper Poison Oak canyon springs, laid several miles of steel pipe, built a reservoir, excavated the hill behind the main house, built on a back porch for the children, and converted the old wine-cellar into a large dining room for entertaining. We built another huge barn. We planted more orchards and built cement posts and fencing to keep the deer from eating the new trees. I invented and fabricated little tin tubes to implant in the cement posts. This enabled us to attach the fencing to the cement posts.

We spent a million dollars, a lot of money in those day, to build what many said was the most beautiful of all ranches. Help was always a problem, but Dad Gould offered to sell his Parkfield Ranch and come down and run Corona del Valle. He was a God-send. He plowed acres of land and planted the hay. He raised the pigs and milk cows and built up a cattle business. Dad Gould terraced the hill and planted more fruit trees and an extensive vegetable garden.

People came from many miles to buy the produce. Grandmother Gould started a chicken and egg business that would supply the busy Sandberg Lodge. With our help, the fields were cleared, the hay planted, mowed and stacked in the barns. The fruit trees were pruned, the fruit picked and

115

marketed. The fences were built, and the wood for the many fireplaces was cut, hauled and stacked. All of this was done with two teams of horses.

I continue my father's story. The period, 1921 until 1929, as a fast-moving and prosperous time for the Robinson family. My folks bought a two-story four-bedroom Mediterranean style home on the corner of Ninth and Linden in downtown Long Beach. Franklin expanded his real-estate holdings to a dozen apartment complexes and doubled the size of the Robinson Hotel. He started the Robinson Williams Insurance Company and bought the Golden State Creamery Company. He immersed himself in civic, church, and social responsibilities. For the first time in his life he was experiencing financial and business success. He tirelessly divided his time between his Long Beach enterprises and the further development of the Corona del Valle Ranch.

I relate a vivid memory I hold of my father. It gives insight into the drive, the tenacity, and the sheer physical endurance of the man. On August 21, 1927, a forest fire started in back of the Sandberg Hotel, three miles west of the ranch. A brisk west wind was blowing. The fire spread rapidly out of control and blasted up the slopes of Liebre Mountain. I had seen the first traces of smoke. The fire storm soon billowed into the sky from the back side of the mountain, but died down after sunset that Sunday night. The county fire service had gotten a few men together to work in confining the fire to the south side of the firebreak, which had been forged out the year before along the entire ridge of Liebre Mountain. All appeared to go well that first night. However, the L.A. County personnel continued to gather several truck loads of men from Los Angeles and brought them to the mountain fire line.

"I know these afternoon winds on the mountain;" my father said. With that, we saddled up the horses and packed water and shovels up the mountain, No sooner had we arrived at the scene than the southwesterly winds prevailed again. The fire erupted! The regenerated flames jumped the firebreak in three places above the ranch, but the recruited unemployed men that had been gathered up in Los Angeles just sat there and watched the fire spread. Pop was furious, but he did not overtly show his anger. Rather, he turned to me and said, "Hold my horse!" Then he called the disorganized men together and had each one take a shovel. The rest of the day and through the night they fought the flames. He drove the men when needed. He encouraged and led by example. He never stopped until all the flames on the north side of the firebreak in back of the ranch were brought under control.

Unfortunately, the fire roared easterly on the south side of the mountain, jumping the fire break again above Three Points. There was another week of raging destruction that took brush, timber, and many dwellings along with it

116

until the inferno burned itself out. The fire had extended from Leibre Gulch and the Ridge Route to the Antelope Valley almond orchards sixteen miles away. It had burned to the Kelly Ranch on the south of the mountain, and to Nenack in the valley to the northeast.

Many said that Franklin Robinson, with a driving energy and a demanding leadership that prevailed in a highly challenging situation, was responsible for saving the north side of the Liebre Mountain from Tent Rock Canyon to Horse Camp Canyon. I believe it, for I saw the fight with my own eyes. Regardless, it was one of the most disastrous burns in the history of Los Angeles County, but not one charred slope could be seen from the Corona del Valle ranch.

Life is never without its victories and defeats, its disasters, sorrows and celebrations. The mark of a man is how he meets the heights and depths of the great adventure. The year 1929 became a time of testing. On October 29 the stock market crashed. Financial panic hit the nation. The dinner conversation around the table that night in our Linden Avenue home in Long Beach was consumed by discussion of this startling development. What would it mean to the expanded real estate obligations Franklin had assumed in the booming economy that was now crumbling?

The economic crash did not immediately put him under. But it did severely shake the confidence of the business community and weakened the financial institutions. The lingering Great Depression, historical in nature, drew the noose tighter and tighter around our family. My father struggled to meet the financial obligations he carried. The oil income kept him in a positive cash flow position for a while, but the pressures kept mounting. He fought to keep the family home. When he was not able to make the payments, the bank foreclosed. Fortunately, he was able to make arrangements to rent, at a reduced rate, until he could reclaim our family home.

One of his finest hours came in 1931, when his oratory won first place in a contest held by the National Association of Real Estate Boards. This winning speech was given in Baltimore, Maryland was entitled, "Long Beach, my Home Town." In the midst of the greatest depression in the history of our nation, he was able to powerfully express his faith in Long Beach and the vision of what the city would become. He practiced the speech with such intensity around the house that I remember many of the phrases from the speech with clarity, One was, "I invite you to Long Beach, the many-sided city of opportunity, the tourist and convention capital of the Pacific Southwest, the hub of industry, commerce and prosperity, a silver strand by a sapphire sea where golden dreams come true."

117

This was a strong statement of faith from a man who had experienced both the booms and the "busts", which were so much a part of early southern California development. Although he had lost much, there was a basic optimism, which was as much a part of him as the air he breathed. There would again be testing in the years that followed.

On March 10, 1933, at 5:55 P.M. a rumbling shattered the calm of the peaceful evening. A second later, the earth heaved and shook for an eternal eleven seconds. The town was in shambles. The outside walls of the St. Marys Hospital, a block away from our home, pealed off and left many of the patients in their beds exposed. Both churches, a block away, collapsed. Mother had been buying ice cream in the drug store across from the hospital. When she felt the quake, she stood still. That saved her life. When the quake stopped, she walked out over the brick and rubble. I saw her coming down the street, walking as if nothing at all had happened. She looked at me and said, "Why are you so white. It's only an earthquake." She and Pop slept in their second story bedroom that night, seemingly unperturbed by the after shocks, even though the house had shifted on the foundation. Long Beach was in chaos

The historic Long Beach earthquake was a final blow for Franklin Robinson. Eventually he lost thirteen apartment houses and the Robinson Hotel and found himself encumbered with a debt of over a half million dollars in a depressed economy. It would be a decade of work and stress before he would be able to pay off the debt. And most of his real estate holdings were gone forever. Fortunately the Corona del Valle Ranch had been refinanced on an emergency government loan at a reduced rate of interest. Franklin could continue to pay the rent on the Linden Avenue home until such time he could redeem it with the oil income.

Still in the midst of the Great Depression, Franklin Robinson suffered great personal losses. John, his esteemed thirty-nine year old younger brother, pastor of the Crescent Height Methodist Church in Hollywood, contracted pneumonia. Less than forty-eight hours later he was dead. It was Easter morning, 1936. The memory is vivid. We had no phones at the ranch in those early days. Mr. Sandberg drove for his Lodge on the summit of the old Ridge Route. Over the cattle guard and up the driveway he came, stopping under the large oak tree in front of our ranch adobe home. It was ten o'clock. I was the only one outside the house. Harold Sandberg got out of his Studebaker convertible touring car. "Better get your dad," he said. When my father came out, Mr. Sandberg said, "Your brother died this morning. His wife (Laureen Buffum Robinson) wanted you to know."

This was another devastating blow to the family. Not only was Uncle John a rising light in the Methodist church, he was the loving father of four

118

wonderful children, all under six years of age. John Wesley Robinson's funeral was held the next week near his boyhood home at the Long Beach First Methodist Church. The service overflowed with those who had come to show their love and respect. Methodist leaders from throughout southern California were there. Following the service, the funeral parade of automobiles drove up Cherry Avenue, over the Signal Hill grade, and to the mausoleum. One could look back and see the long line of cars that stretched from Signal Hill to the Pacific Ocean at Bixby Park.

Less than a year later his father, John Wesley Robinson (Sr.), died suddenly of nephritis, a kidney disease. Franklin went north to Berkeley, California for his father's body and returned to Los Angeles on the Southern Pacific train. I remember greeting my father at the terminal and watching the train crew unload my grandfather's coffin from the express car. He was interned at the Robinson family plot in the Evergreen Cemetery in East Los Angeles. My grandfather's last trip was on the route he had made many times in his evangelistic preaching up and down the state of California.

Franklin deeply felt the loss of his entire birth family, which he outlived for some forty years. While teaching a class at the Grace Methodist Church one Sunday morning, the realization of loss and aloneness swept uncontrollably over him. He could not stop the weeping, left, and walked the streets of Long Beach until it was somehow resolved.

*   *   *

The World War II years were hard for my parents. They showed four blue stars in the window of the Linden Avenue home. Each blue star designated one of their three boys and a son-in-law who were involved in the conflict. They hoped always that none of us would be lost, that never would one of those stars have to be changed to gold. My mother spent extended periods in the desert during those desperate times. It was her way of coping. It was an escape from the realities of the war-torn world she was experiencing. In 1943 my father provided a one-room cabin for her in Desert Hot Springs. It became her retreat. She later wrote:

I lived in a one-room cabin in Desert Hot Springs and have no doubt that the spring was, as old-timers said, the windiest they had ever experienced. The wind would pick up sand and gravel and throw it against the windows, setting up such a clatter that I could imagine myself a thousand miles from any habitation.

But the wind did not blow every day. There were times when it was breathlessly still. The sun was mild and warm and the tiny flowers opened, carpeting the desert, white, pink, and yellow. I would face Mt. San Jacinto, a sheer granite monument capped with snow. Through the pass into the Los Angeles basin long trains moved day after day, carrying materials for war. Overhead airplane motors throbbed, muted by the distance. The war was in full swing with all of its destruction and killing. But day-by-day, it all grew more and more impersonal to me. When I came to the desert, I was weary with the world. Now I was a captive of the wind, the sand, and the rock. I was finding a peace.

This was a difficult time for my father, too. Although there was a great love between my parents, there were great differences in their needs and personalities. She was an introspective intellectual, while he was a person of action and drive. If he were to spend some time in the desert with her, he needed a project. So he bought a large parcel of land on the northwest outskirts of Desert Hot Springs to develop. The price of land was reasonable, because no one had been able to get enough water for a project. This did not deter my father. He went up to the old ranch and drove Dad Gould back to Desert Hot Springs to "witch" for water. Dad Gould had located many successful wells throughout the state with a willow switch. My father had more confidence in his ability to locate water than any of the professionals. It didn't take Dad Gould long to locate a good stream, which he said ran under the property. Franklin was not surprised when the water came with abundance. He immediately founded a little water company. Now he had more than an adequate supply of water for the Cholla Gardens development in Desert Hot Springs.

Immediately, he built a new home on a view site. The family remembers many wonderful breakfast mornings on our parent's flagstone porch, talking and enjoying the spectacular view from out across the high desert to the shear granite face of Mt. San Jacinto.

My mother took great pride in restoring the natural desert around their home. She and Pop would wait for members of the family to arrive. Then they had all of us work with long pipe fulcrums to lift the large, partially-sand-submerged boulders from the ground for all to see and enjoy. Many times the work was the price for our Thanksgiving dinner.

Sadly, this period of Franklin's life ended when Hope died in the late summer of 1958. This began his twenty-year adjustment to life without his chosen mate. But it was never a part of his nature to give up. He sold all of his holdings in Desert Hot Springs and moved to Palm Springs to develop a luxurious condominium on Via Lola, called Villa de las Palmas. This project was a complex deal for a man of any age to put together. But he prevailed! Eventually he gained control of the property and built the Palm Springs condominium structure of his dreams. A choice apartment, of his choosing, became his primary home for the next twelve years.

Living in Palm Springs, with his proximity to the O'Donnell Country Club, to which he could drive his golf cart, gave him the opportunity to maintain his outstanding golfing ability. He was devoted to the game. During those years, Franklin Robinson earned the title of Mr. Senior Golf. He won the National Seniors Tournament. In that final championship round, held at the famous Thunderbird Country Club, he won by firing an even par 71, at the age of 71.

The next year he won the California State Championship, the Palm Springs Desert Senior Tournament, and successfully defended his National Senior's title. This phenomenal record entitled him to a new title, Grand Slam Senior Champion! Asked for the secret of his success, he said, "I am an incurable 'golfaholic.' I love the game. I love the out of doors. I seem to thrive on competition and I find there is nothing equal to the good fellowship of like-minded men who get together for a friendly game on a beautiful golf course." When recuperating from a serious cancer operation in 1973, he said, "All I want is at least five more years to be with my buddies at the Virginia Country Club." He got his wish.

On the morning of April 19, 1978, on his own initiative, he got into his big old Chrysler automobile and drove himself to the Long Beach Memorial Hospital. The family did not know where he was. Finally, Dr. Stephen Van Camp, his grand son-in-law, found his car in the hospital parking lot. Mystery solved!

On the morning of May 2, 1978, Franklin Robinson died of cancer. Joan Robinson, my wife and his daughter-in-law flew from Houston, Texas to spend those last days with him. Joan had the priceless opportunity to listen, as he reviewed his life. There was a special bond between Joan and our father. He was able to speak freely of his last concerns, the love for his family, and finally the resolution of the biblical truth, with which he had struggled. He left in peace.

Shortly after, his brother-in-law, Phil Gould distributed Franklin's ashes, as he had requested, from an airplane over the north face of Mt. San Jacinto Symbolically, his remains floated gently to join those of his wife, Hope Gould Robinson. It brought back memories. Seventeen years before, I had written:

Before dawn, my brother Ted and I drove to the base of San Jacinto, the mountain that had given our mother solace during the difficult times in

World War II. High on the granite face there was a large outcropping of white quartz. It took the form of a giant angel, dramatically spreading its wings across the escarpment—the Angel of San Jacinto. Our parents had pointed it out many times from their home in Desert Hot Springs.

Ted and I parked the car in the dark at the base of the mountain and slowly worked our way up a rock ridge. We surmised, this would take us to the top of the angel's spread wings. We apprehensively climbed through the darkness of a delayed dawn, created by a blanket of clouds, which had moved against the mountain. Two hours later, the sky began to lighten. A few more rocks to scale--then we broke out through the overcast into an indescribable world of light. A hundred yards to our left glowed the white outstretched wings of the angel. We looked down into the rock gorge below, from which the monumental body of the divine figure ascended. Lovingly, Ted scattered our mother's earthly remains along the outstretched wings, as if the angel were preparing for flight. Ted and I sat silently for a moment. The sky and the earth had opened. To the east, we faced a new and vivid sunrise, which now lighted our mother's beloved desert. In a way, we had committed Hope Gould Robinson "to the assured theological hope of eternal adventure," the gift and mystery of life.

Our parent's desire and commitment to be with one another, now expressed symbolically on the Angel Wings of San Jacinto, hopefully will bring solace, hope, and commitment to those who follow.

The memorial service for our father, Franklin Willard Robinson, was held a week after his death. Members of the family from as far away as Oregon and Texas had made the journey to the family's favorite knoll in the pines above the original old Corona del Valle ranch. The knoll, to the west, dropped off into Robinson Canyon, which had been named for our father by directors of the Angeles National Forest. This beautiful canyon was forested with the rare towering Big Cone Spruce, a majestic tree indigenous only to selected areas of the Sierra Madre Mountains in southern California.

It was late spring. Looking over the Antelope valley, the golden poppies carpeted the desert floor and the foothills of the Tehachapi range. The mountain lilac was in full bloom. Bees were busy with their work. New life was all around. Those in attendance walked together up the mountain and gathered for the service. There was a guitar, a gifted voice, the familiar hymns, appropriate and assuring scriptures, and the sharing of memories, as each placed a juniper cutting at the base of the cross. With our grief, there was thanksgiving and celebration.

On May 16, 1978, the <u>Press Telegram</u>, Long Beach's daily newspaper, published this article on the life of Franklin W. Robinson:

Some men look at the needs of a city and ask helplessly, "Why doesn't somebody do something?" Other men roll up their sleeves and answer the question with their labors. No community can flourish without its doers, the hard workers who translate visions into accomplishments for the common good. Franklin Robinson was one of the doers. A man who got much from life, but returned the gifts he received in full measure. He built apartments, hotels, residences, and made money in oil investments. He was vice president of the Chamber of Commerce, and a tireless worker in the World War 1 relief campaign. He was an active member of Kiwanis International and supporter of the Boy Scout Council.

When the Y.M.C.A. needed a prime mover for its expansion drive, or the Methodist Church needed a financial campaign director for a building project, Franklin Robinson was there. When the Community Chest needed an extra push, he took over as general chairman of the fund drive. When the time came to build the new civic auditorium and pier developments, he headed the campaign. He was the civic leader for putting Long Beach in as a member of the Metropolitan Water District and led a successful and heated campaign to bring much needed Colorado River water for the future growth of the city.

He was the General Chairman of the Christmas Seal drive. Franklin Robinson was a member of the 1932 Long Beach division of the American Olympic Committee, which organized the rowing and sailing activities of the Olympic Games. (Participants of these events were housed in the Robinson Hotel on Ocean Boulevard.)

Franklin Robinson was a pioneer in the development of the Port of Long Beach and the man who headed up the Red Cross relief effort after the 1933 earthquake. He served for sixteen years as a member of the Long Beach Board of Education, serving two terms as the President. He was elected President of the Virginia Country Club. The list goes on and on. Whenever the city had a task to be done, Franklin Robinson was available for duty.

A FINAL TRIBUTE

(Written by Franklin Willard Robinson Jr. for his fathers memorial service, May 1978)

Our father is an unique person, a complex balance of the tender, the material, the searching and the certain. Should one select adjectives in an attempt to describe this lovable man, tenacious and loyal would have to be included. His loyalty to his wife, to the family, and all he loved would have to be included. He had the courage to commit to any difficult task and the tenacity to see it through. He modeled a solidity of purpose. Because of this, those who have been touched by him meet life with a little more assurance, a little more fight and a little more toughness of resolve. He encouraged us to launch forth, pursue our individual stars without restraints or controlling manipulation from him. He was the model patriarch. In this respect he modeled the God/person relationship ... a constant and supporting love, with the blessing to go free in personal decision and independence of action. There was never a need to rebel.

Our father also gave us the gift of a questioning spirit. We lived with him in a reverent questioning of the infinite truths he could not deny and yet could not fully understand. There was integrity in this life-long struggle, which those who are spiritually oriented will relate to with compassion and love. He gave us the blessing to creatively pursue the world of position and achievement, but always within the moral and ethical context of the religious culture with which he had been ingrained.

We have seen Pop expend physical and emotional energy, as he has partaken and given throughout a lifetime that was rich and blessed with many years. He sensed an understandable tiredness. This, he had no recourse but to accept. For this good man, we too must accept. But it is painful, for he is our father.

FRANKLIN W. ROBINSON
1901

Age 11, Long Beach, California

FRANKLIN W. ROBINSON 1909

Student at U.S.C.

ROBINSON HOTEL
LONG BEACH, CALIFORNIA
1918

Built by Franklin W. Robinson and first called "The Sutherland"

The Sutherland was built on Ocean Ave during World War I and later renamed Robinson Hotel in the early 1920's. During the 1932 Olympics the hotel housed participants in the rowing and sailing events

127

RANCHO CORONA DEL VALLE
July 4, 1933

Franklin Robinson addressing Long Beach Oxford group leaders under the huge oak in front of his ranch home.

During the 1930's, Franklin Robinson invited Long Beach community groups. in which he was involved, to the ranch for hospitality, fellowship and training. These groups included the Long Beach Chamber of Commerce, Oxford Group members and leaders, his Grace Methodist Sunday School class, and Alumni Reunions of his 1905 graduating class from Long Beach Polytechnic High School.

FRANKLIN W. ROBINSON FAMILY
Christmas 1940

At home at 858 Linden Ave., Long Beach, California
From left to right: Franklin, Rosamond, Ted,
Charles, Willard, and Hope (Gould) Robinson

RANCH HOUSE at RANCHO CORONA del VALLE
1942 – 1946

Living Room of the Robinson Ranch House: Adobe Hacienda

For twenty-years, the Franklin Robinson family celebrated their Christmas in this magnificent ranch living room. Huge oak logs in the massive fireplace heated the room. The early American furniture, decorative Navajo Indian rugs, antiques, and baskets were originally purchased through the famous Mission Inn, Riverside, California, in 1920. The Navajo rugs, as seen in the picture, still cover the rich Bachelor Tile floors. The beams are solid redwood and the ceiling is of redwood planks.

The Spanish hacienda forms a "U" around an enclosed patio area. There are four fireplaces, two of them made from original adobe blocks from the ruins of the famous Fort Tejon. The home can sleep a dozen people, and was the hospitality center for many occasions.

FRANKLIN W. ROBINSON
1968 at age 79

PARENTS OF FRANKLIN WILLARD ROBINSON

John W. Robinson, Age 30   **Rosamond Burnett, Age 22**

Born October 10, 1855,
    Albion, Iowa.
Married 1886.
Died November, 1936,
    Berkeley, California.

Born 1863,
    Nacimiento, California.
Married 1886.
Died 1918,
    Long Beach, California.

Both parents are buried in the Evergreen Cemetery, Los Angeles, California.

GENEALOGY OF FRANKLIN W. ROBINSON

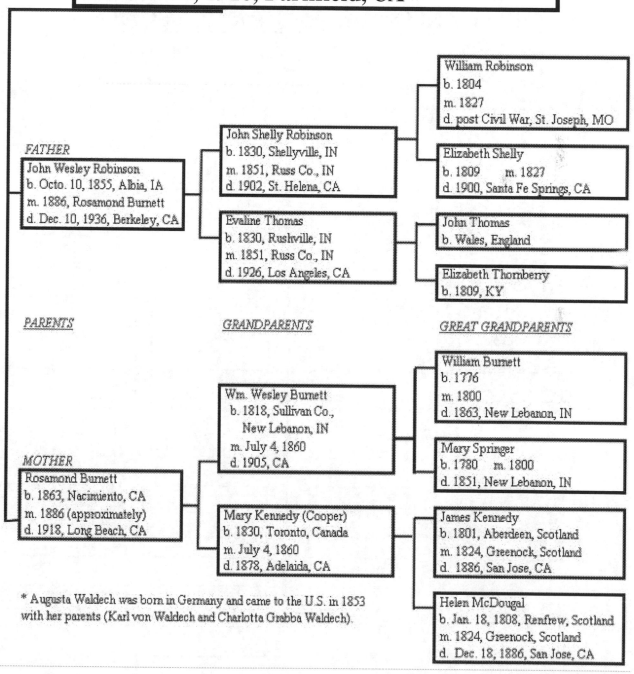

Franklin Willard Robinson
b. May 27, 1889, Grainsville, Kings Co., CA
m. Oct. 31, 1916, Parkfield, CA

FATHER

John Wesley Robinson
b. Octo. 10, 1855, Albia, IA
m. 1886, Rosamond Burnett
d. Dec. 10, 1936, Berkeley, CA

John Shelly Robinson
b. 1830, Shellyville, IN
m. 1851, Russ Co., IN
d. 1902, St. Helena, CA

William Robinson
b. 1804
m. 1827
d. post Civil War, St. Joseph, MO

Elizabeth Shelly
b. 1809   m. 1827
d. 1900, Santa Fe Springs, CA

Evaline Thomas
b. 1830, Rushville, IN
m. 1851, Russ Co., IN
d. 1926, Los Angeles, CA

John Thomas
b. Wales, England

Elizabeth Thornberry
b. 1809, KY

PARENTS   *GRANDPARENTS*   *GREAT GRANDPARENTS*

Wm. Wesley Burnett
b. 1818, Sullivan Co.,
   New Lebanon, IN
m. July 4, 1860
d. 1905, CA

William Burnett
b. 1776
m. 1800
d. 1863, New Lebanon, IN

Mary Springer
b. 1780   m. 1800
d. 1851, New Lebanon, IN

MOTHER

Rosamond Burnett
b. 1863, Nacimiento, CA
m. 1886 (approximately)
d. 1918, Long Beach, CA

Mary Kennedy (Cooper)
b. 1830, Toronto, Canada
m. July 4, 1860
d. 1878, Adelaida, CA

James Kennedy
b. 1801, Aberdeen, Scotland
m. 1824, Greenock, Scotland
d. 1886, San Jose, CA

Helen McDougal
b. Jan. 18, 1808, Renfrew, Scotland
m. 1824, Greenock, Scotland
d. Dec. 18, 1886, San Jose, CA

* Augusta Waldech was born in Germany and came to the U.S. in 1853
with her parents (Karl von Waldech and Charlotta Grabba Waldech).

DESCENDENTS OF FRANKLIN
AND HOPE ROBINSON

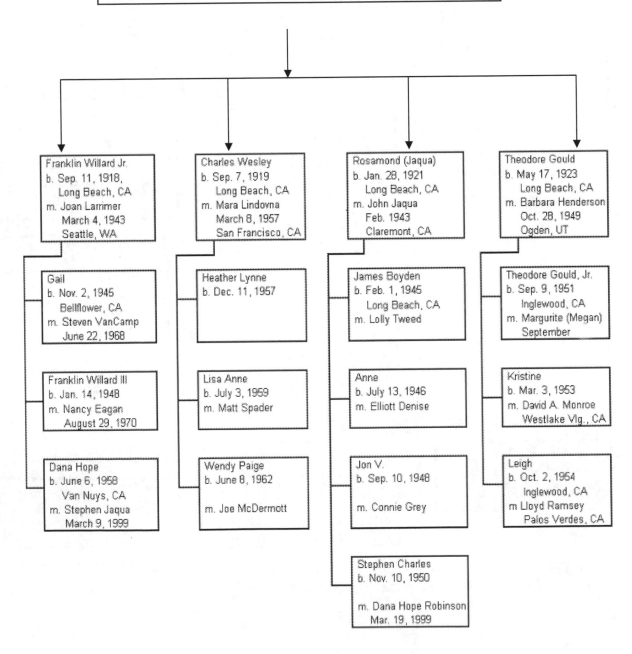

Franklin W. Robinson 1889-1978
Hope Gould Robinson 1893-1958
married October 31   Parkfield, CA

Franklin Willard Jr.
b. Sep. 11, 1918,
   Long Beach, CA
m. Joan Larrimer
   March 4, 1943
   Seattle, WA

Charles Wesley
b. Sep. 7, 1919
   Long Beach, CA
m. Mara Lindovna
   March 8, 1957
   San Francisco, CA

Rosamond (Jaqua)
b. Jan. 28, 1921
   Long Beach, CA
m. John Jaqua
   Feb. 1943
   Claremont, CA

Theodore Gould
b. May 17, 1923
   Long Beach, CA
m. Barbara Henderson
   Oct. 28, 1949
   Ogden, UT

Gail
b. Nov. 2, 1945
   Bellflower, CA
m. Steven VanCamp
   June 22, 1968

Heather Lynne
b. Dec. 11, 1957

James Boyden
b. Feb. 1, 1945
   Long Beach, CA
m. Lolly Tweed

Theodore Gould, Jr.
b. Sep. 9, 1951
   Inglewood, CA
m. Margurite (Megan)
   September

Franklin Willard III
b. Jan. 14, 1948
m. Nancy Eagan
   August 29, 1970

Lisa Anne
b. July 3, 1959
m. Matt Spader

Anne
b. July 13, 1946
m. Elliott Denise

Kristine
b. Mar. 3, 1953
m. David A. Monroe
   Westlake Vlg., CA

Dana Hope
b. June 6, 1958
   Van Nuys, CA
m. Stephen Jaqua
   March 9, 1999

Wendy Paige
b. June 8, 1962

m. Joe McDermott

Jon V.
b. Sep. 10, 1948

m. Connie Grey

Leigh
b. Oct. 2, 1954
   Inglewood, CA
m Lloyd Ramsey
   Palos Verdes, CA

Stephen Charles
b. Nov. 10, 1950

m. Dana Hope Robinson
   Mar. 19, 1999

GRANDCHILDREN & GREAT GRANDCHILDREN
Franklin W. & Hope G. Robinson

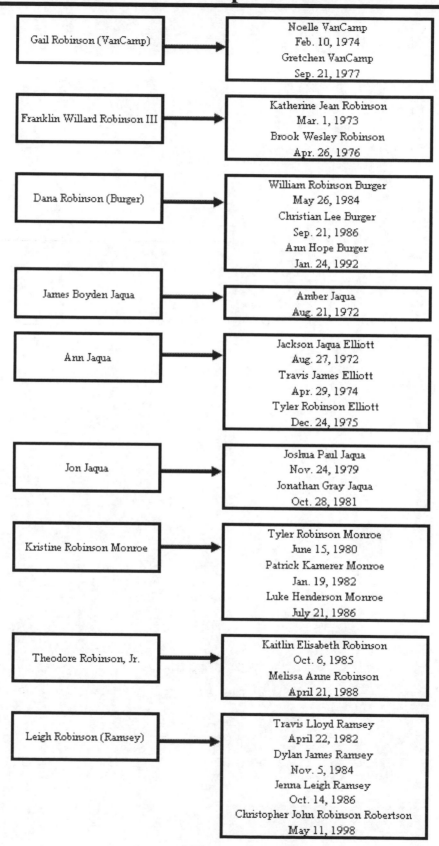

Gail Robinson (VanCamp)	Noelle VanCamp Feb. 10, 1974 Gretchen VanCamp Sep. 21, 1977
Franklin Willard Robinson III	Katherine Jean Robinson Mar. 1, 1973 Brook Wesley Robinson Apr. 26, 1976
Dana Robinson (Burger)	William Robinson Burger May 26, 1984 Christian Lee Burger Sep. 21, 1986 Ann Hope Burger Jan. 24, 1992
James Boyden Jaqua	Amber Jaqua Aug. 21, 1972
Ann Jaqua	Jackson Jaqua Elliott Aug. 27, 1972 Travis James Elliott Apr. 29, 1974 Tyler Robinson Elliott Dec. 24, 1975
Jon Jaqua	Joshua Paul Jaqua Nov. 24, 1979 Jonathan Gray Jaqua Oct. 28, 1981
Kristine Robinson Monroe	Tyler Robinson Monroe June 15, 1980 Patrick Kamerer Monroe Jan. 19, 1982 Luke Henderson Monroe July 21, 1986
Theodore Robinson, Jr.	Kaitlin Elisabeth Robinson Oct. 6, 1985 Melissa Anne Robinson April 21, 1988
Leigh Robinson (Ramsey)	Travis Lloyd Ramsey April 22, 1982 Dylan James Ramsey Nov. 5, 1984 Jenna Leigh Ramsey Oct. 14, 1986 Christopher John Robinson Robertson May 11, 1998

135

THE JOAN LARRIMER FAMILY HISTORY

Genealogy of the Beckwith Family in France and England,
1138 to Establishment in America in 1635

Genealogy of the Matthew Beckwith Family,
1635 to Ethel Beckwith (Larrimer) 1950

The Joan L. Robinson Life Story

INTRODUCTION TO
THE JOAN LARRIMER FAMILY IN AMERICA

Research on the lineage of the Joan Robinson family began in 1947, following World War II. Joan and I built a home in North Hollywood, California. Gail was born in 1945, and Tri (Franklin Willard Robinson III) in 1948. Joan and I began working on their baby books, and realized that we had limited knowledge of the Larrimer lineage. In talking with Joan's parents, we were able to go back for three generations, but specific information on the family remained sparse. We were able to build a family tree for the children, which went back four generations, but the details of these ancestors lives remained a mystery.

While living in Kerrville, Texas from 1975, until 1982, we began to research and gather information for a family history. Through the genealogical records available in various libraries, we were eventually able to establish that lines of both the Robinson and Larrimer families were listed as founders of Watersford, Connecticut, in 1639. In the Larrimer line, it was Mathew Beckwith (Joan's mother was a Beckwith). In the Robinson line, it was Josiah Churchill (my Grandmother, May Gould was a Churchill). Our mutual ancestor, Josiah, arrived in Watersford, Connecticut, from England in 1635.

Once this had been established, we made contact with ancestral organizations and obtained extended research material. An example from the Kerrville Library: <u>Beckwith</u>, See History of Seymour Family, FAM 19 p.166. Weatherford, Conn. Will of Slias Seymour of Weathersfield, dated 23 Jan 1721 names son-in-law Seth Beckwith, etc.

It was a giant game that led from one piece of the puzzle to another. We located a distant cousin of Joan's who had done extensive family research. Cousin May Beckwith Jackson, of Toledo, Ohio, wrote in part:

Dear Cousin Joan,
You mentioned in your letter "Beckwith Notes," by Albert C. Beckwith. I had never heard of this document, so I went to Fort Myers, Indiana yesterday and looked it up. It proved to be a valuable history of the family. I will mail you a copy. Sincerely, May Beckwith Jackson

It is interesting. Over the years, in Joan's line, we have established twenty-six uninterrupted generations, which span almost two thousand years of history. Read with wonder and appreciation. *F. Willard Robinson*

RELATIONSHIP OF THE JOAN ROBINSON FAMILY TO THE BECKWITH FAMLY LINEAGE IN AMERICA

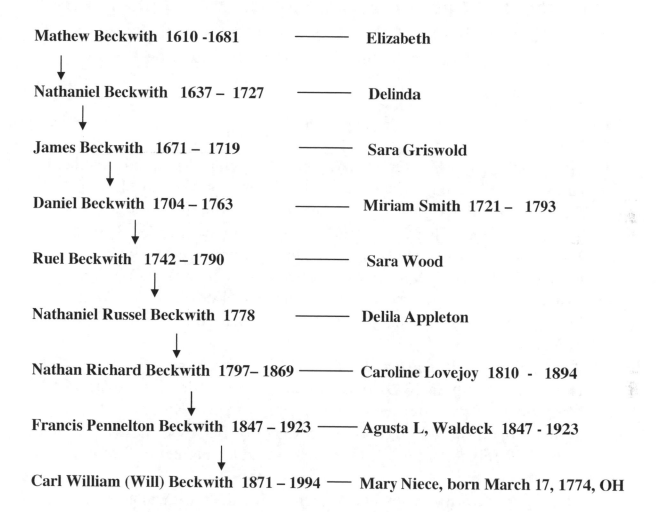

Mathew Beckwith 1610 -1681 ——— Elizabeth

Nathaniel Beckwith 1637 – 1727 ——— Delinda

James Beckwith 1671 – 1719 ——— Sara Griswold

Daniel Beckwith 1704 – 1763 ——— Miriam Smith 1721 – 1793

Ruel Beckwith 1742 – 1790 ——— Sara Wood

Nathaniel Russel Beckwith 1778 ——— Delila Appleton

Nathan Richard Beckwith 1797– 1869 ——— Caroline Lovejoy 1810 - 1894

Francis Pennelton Beckwith 1847 – 1923 ——— Agusta L, Waldeck 1847 - 1923

Carl William (Will) Beckwith 1871 – 1994 —— Mary Niece, born March 17, 1774, OH

Children of Carl (Will) Beckwith and Mary Niece:
Ethel Beckwith (Larrimer)
Georgia Beckwith (Farren)
Jessie Beckwith (Hughes)

Children of Ethel Beckwith (Larrimer):
Mary Helen Larrimer (Hoskin)
Joan Larrimer (Robinson)

GENEALOGICAL RECORD OF THE BECKWITH FAMILY

From 1138, Normandy, France; then England until 1619, when the first Beckwiths came to America; followed by eleven generations of the Beckwith family in America.
(From the letter of May Beckwith Jackson)

From 1138 until 1619

- Lord of Mathleye.
- Sir Hercules De MSir Hugh De Malebisse. Born in Normandy and held lands with William the Conquerer in the County of York in 1138.
- Sir Rugo De Malebisse Married daughter of William de Percy.
- Sir Simon De Malebisse Lord of Cowton in Craven Married daughter of John Lalebisse. He changed his name to Beckwith in 1226, on his marriage to to Lady Dame Beckwith Bruce, daughter of Sir William Bruce of Uglebarley,, who was a descendant of Lord Bruce of Scotland.
- Sir Hercules Beckwith married daughter of Sir John Ferrers of Tamsworth Castle.
- Nicholas Beckwith married daughter of Sir John Chaworth
- Hamon Beckwith, in 1339, took the coat of arms of John, Lord De Malaebisse. He married a daughter of Philip Tynley Knight.
- William Beckwith was second of the Manor of Beckwithshow in the 38th year of the reign of Edward, 1364 He married a daughter of Sir Girard Urfleet.
- Thomas Beckwith of Olint and Manors of Magna Otrigen and Housely, near Churshy, married daughter of John Sawly of Saxon.
- Adam Beckwith De Clint married Elizabeth De Malebisse,
- Sir William Beckwith De Clint. Married daughter of Sir John Baskerville.
- Thomas Beckwith o\De Clint, Lord of one third part of Filey, Muster and Thorp, married the daughter and heiress of William Heslerton.
- John Beckwith married the daughter of Thomas Radcliffe of Mulgrave.
- Robert Beckwith of Broxholme was living in the 8th year of King Edward IV.
- John Beckwith of Clint and Thorp, was living in the 8th year of Edward

- Robert Beckwith of Clint and Thor, married Jennet.
- Marmaduke Beckwith, of Darce and Clint, married 2nd. Anne, daughter of Dynly of Bramhope, County of York.

From 1619 to 1944

- Mathew Beckwith, born Sept. 22, 1610, Pontefract. Yorkshire, England. Migrated in 1635 to New England, residing for a time at Saybrook Point, 1635, then to Bradford, 1638. He was then with the first settlers of Hartford, Connecticut, 1642, and then to Lyme where in 1651 he purchased large tracts of land on the Nantic River from Lyme to New London. He then built the barque *Endeaver*. This was the first sailing ship ever launched from New London, Connecticut. His ship traded goods from the Barbados Islands. He died, a wealthy man, on December 13, 1681. At the time of his death, his wife's Christian name was Elizabeth
- Nathanial Beckwith was born in 1637 at Saybrook Point, Connecticut. His birth was recorded at Waterford. In his adult years, he lived in Guilford, Connecticut, where he became one of the founders of the church, where he later served as a deacon. Nathan died at New London, June 4, 1727. He, like his father Mathew, became a renowned seaman. He was married twice and had eight children by his first first wife. Records show that tragedy hit the family. One of his boys, Joseph, was killed in the French and Indian War, 1706. Another son, Benjamin, became a mariner and was lost at sea. Fortunately, Nathanial's son Joseph continued the family line that made the present Robinson/Larrimer lineage possible.
- Joseph Beckwith was born June 1, 1671 in New London, Connecticut. He married Sara Griswold on September 22, 1693. They raised nine children, one of which, Daniel Beckwith, was Joan Robinson's direct ancestor. Daniel Beckwith died in 1719 at Lyme, Connecticut.
- Daniel Beckwith was born on October 26. 1744 in Lyme, Connecticut. He married Miriam Smith. They had eight children, one of which was Ruel Beckwith, the direct ancestor of Joan Larrimer Robinson. During Daniel's life,\ he was a farmer and a Baptist minister. Daniel Beckwith died, November 10, 1763, in Lyme, Connnecticut.
- Ruel Beckwith was born on August 18, 1742 in Lyme, Connecticut. He married Sara Woodon December 9, 1773, and to them were born seven children, one of whom was Nathaniel Beckwith. Ruel Beckwith died in

141

Lyme on December 11, 1775.

- <u>Nathaniel Russel Beckwith</u> was born September 12, 1179 in Lyme, Connecticut. His wife's name was Dalinda, and to them were born seven children, the oldest of whom was a boy, Nathan Richard. Records indicate that Nathanial died in in Oswego, New York.

- <u>Nathan Richard</u> Beckwith was born in Oswego. New York on February 26, 1797. Records do not indicate the name of his first wife, or the circumstances of her death. It is known that Nathan married again. His second wife. Carolyn was thirteen years younger than Nathan, that her name was Caroline, and to them were born four children, the oldest of whom was Francis Pennelton.

- <u>Francis Pennelton Beckwith</u> was born, April 4, 1847, some say in Watertown, New York. We do know that as a young lad he came to the Toledo, Ohio area about 1860 and joined the Union Army for a two year enlistment in the Civil War. Following the war he served as a member of the Toledo Fire Department for six years, and served in the Court House. Francis, or Frank as he was called, married Agusta L. Waldeck in Toledo, December 18, 1864. Augusta was born in the principality of Waldeck, Germany, July 15, 1847 and came to this country in 1853 with her parents, Karl (Von) Waldeck and Carlotta Grabba Waldeck.

- Francis and Agusta had four children, one of whom was Carl William (Will) Beckwith, who became the grandfather of Joan Larrimer (Robinson)

- Francis P. Beckwith died in Toledo, Ohio, June 20, 1923. Agusta died in Toledo, October 20, 1923. This venerable couple were buried in Willow Cemetery, East Toledo, Ohio.

- <u>Carl William (Will) Beckwith</u> was born March 1, 1871 , Toledo, Ohio. He married Mary Niece . They had three daughters: Ethel Beckwith Larrimer, Georgia Beckwith Farren, and Jessie Beckwith Hughes.. Unfortunately, Will Beckwith abandoned his family, while living in Anderson, Indiana. He was later divorced, and died in Newport, Kentucky on January 4, 1944.

JOAN LARRIMER ROBINSON
Born December 10, 1921

I first became aware of Joan Larrimer when she was in the tenth grade at Long Beach Polytechnic High School, and I was a senior. Poly had an enrollment of 3,000 students, but even in such a large, prestigious school, this vivacious, attractive, and excellent student soon became a recognized leader on campus. We first met when, as a senior debate team member, I was asked to moderate a tenth-grade debate held before a civic organization meeting at the Lakewood Country Club in Long Beach, California. Following the debate, I asked Joan if I could drive her home. She was fifteen years old.

When Joan was twenty-one, we were married in Seattle, Washington. That was March 4, 1943. Our life together during those months of World War II, like so many others' lives during that difficult, uncertain and challenging time was unique, to say the least. Joan's courage, loyalty, and love gave me a steady mooring as I plied the rough seas of separation, anxiety, uncertainty, danger and loneliness during World War II. She has been there for me for what has now been sixty-four years of marriage. Here is the story Joan tells.

*   *   *

I was born in Anderson, Indiana on December 10, 1921. My father was Lee Larrimer and my mother was Ethel Beckwith Larrimer. I had a sister, Mary Helen Larrimer (Hoskin), who was four years older. There was also an older half-sister, Virginia Larrimer (Lee). I didn't get to know her very well until later in life, when I was grown and she married Howard Lee. After my father's divorce she had lived with grandmother and grandfather Larrimer. My mother and Virginia didn't get along too well, so we could not see each other often in those early years.

143

I came to Long Beach, California, on a train with my four-year-old sister, my mother and my father. I was only seven weeks old. Of course I don't remember anything about the time in Anderson, nor the train trip to California, but I do know it was an adventure for our family. As part of his research for family history, Robbie and I drove across the country in 1994. We stopped in Anderson, Indiana. I was curious about the place where I was born. We did find some valuable information on the Beckwith and Larrimer families in the Anderson Library. However, I am glad I didn't spend my life in Anderson, Indiana.

Looking back, I would describe my family as poor, although I didn't think too much about that during the time I was growing up. We were in the middle of the greatest depression of all time, but so many of my friends were in the same position. As children we took a lot of things for granted. The fact is, the Great Depression did hit our family very hard. We lost our home and had to rent a small house for $25 per month. We planted a little garden, like a lot of people did, along the Los Angeles Riverbed. Dad couldn't get a steady job. So my mother, who was an excellent seamstress, made costumes for skaters in the Ice Follies. This kept us going. Mother appeared strong, controlled and responsible. In fact she was a very talented woman, who suffered from the insecurities in her life. Out of this basic fear, she found comfort and meaning in Christian Science (CS). Even as a small child, I felt uncomfortable with this, and resisted going to the CS Sunday school.

Fortunately, I was blessed when I was in elementary school by a special lady who took an interest in me and several of my girlfriends. Her name was Renna Cooper. We called her Miss Cooper, and I shall never forget her. I don't remember exactly how this happened, but Miss Cooper met with us each week in a little Baptist church in our neighborhood. She told us about Jesus, read Bible stories, and we had refreshments. I remember how loved and cared for we felt. This was my first sense of Christian community. This early childhood experience did build a foundation for my continued search to know more about Jesus and the "Kingdom of God."

We went to the Burnett Elementary School on Atlantic Boulevard in Long Beach. This was interesting, because I found out later that the school was named after Peter B. Burnett, the first governor of California, and a distant cousin of the Robinson family. I had no idea then that I would someday be a relative of an historic governor.

My most vivid memory of elementary school took place one day late in the afternoon. I was playing on the high bar. An oil refinery, not too many blocks away on Signal Hill, blew up. The explosion knocked me off the high bar. I was dazed! That same year, on March 10, 1933, the Long Beach earthquake wrecked the town. All of this was enough to make a little girl anxious. I graduated from elementary school that same year.

Hamilton Junior High was the school I attended for the next three years. I have few memories of the time, other than walking the thirteen blocks to and from school with my friends. I learned to play the cello and carried the huge instrument back and forth every day. I played in the orchestra. Too, on occasion, I walked the two miles to the beach with my friends to play and swim in the surf. My folks never worried about us. Long Beach was a wonderful place to live.

In 1936 I left junior high and entered Long Beach Polytechnic High School. To move into a school of 3,000 could be daunting for some, but I was fortunate to have a number of great friends, one of whom was Jean Huron. We hit it off right away and decided to run for the varsity football song leading team. It was unheard of for tenth graders to run for this position. Jean and I decided to run anyway—and we won.

Long Beach Poly football was a major event in Long Beach. What wonderful memories I have. You could not run for song leader two years in a row, but we were elected again in our senior year. Long Beach Poly won the CIF championship in 1939, beating Glendale High School in the Rose Bowl before a crowd of 40,000. We led songs and yells with our pompoms flying. All of this activity enabled us to be known on campus, opening the doors for elected office and public speaking opportunities. Our academic records were admirable and our social life full. It was the era of the "Big Bands," and we danced almost every week. The years 1936 to 1939 remain a highlight in my life. But two years later World War II began.

*   *   *

On December 7, 1941, Japan attacked Pearl Harbor. This traumatic event hit me with an emotional impact that, to this day, I can still feel. The anger and shock still cause me pain. My twentieth birthday was three days away. I was completing my study at Long Beach Junior College, but my future looked bleak, vague and frightening. The Great Depression that started in 1929 was still lingering in 1941. It had been a desperate twelve years for my parents as they fought to simply endure. We were like so many others, struggling through the Depression's deprivations: lost jobs, lost homes and lost hope. On top of this, we would now face a tragic global war.

I finished school and applied for work at the Cherry Avenue Branch of the First Security National Bank in Long Beach, California. I was elated to get the job and started working immediately. The bank was without experienced personnel. When war was declared, all the men left to join the armed forces. Mr. Brown, the Branch Manager, was left to run the bank with untrained, very young women. My salary was eighteen dollars a week. I knew nothing about the banking business, but I spent over fifty hours a week working and learning. It is a wonder the entire banking world didn't sink, never to recover, from this influx of inexperienced workers. But somehow we did prevail, and I found personal satisfaction in knowing I was doing something necessary for the continued stability of our country in a time of great need. I worked at the bank for about twelve months, proud that I was able to reconcile the books at the close of each banking day.

At that point in time, Ensign F. Willard "Robbie" Robinson came back into my life. I hadn't seen or heard from Robbie for at least two years. When he came unexpectedly into the bank and asked me to have dinner with him, I was very surprised. However, we had known each other and had dated off and on in the earlier days of our acquaintance. We had always cared for one another, but dating was difficult. So, we went out to dinner that February night in 1943. We talked through the circumstances of our lives during the many months we had been apart. Then it was time to go. He drove back to my parent's house and as he was ready to leave he dumbfounded me.

"I'm leaving for Seattle the first thing in the morning to join my new torpedo squadron, which is being commissioned at the Sand Point Naval Air Station," he began. "Will you come to Seattle and marry me? It is a big decision, so don't answer me now. I will call you in three days, and if you will come, I'll send you a train ticket and make all the arrangements."

When he called me three days later, I told him I would come. I knew, of course, that my friends would look upon this decision as impulsive, but I felt very sure and right about our marriage. Robbie and I would have whatever time together the risks of war would allow. We wanted this. We laugh now, sixty-five years later, and remark, "It was an impulsive war marriage that may still work out." Anyway, Robbie was fortunate enough to get a train ticket to Seattle. I say fortunate, because during the war, travel was almost exclusively reserved for servicemen. When the day for my departure arrived, my folks drove me to the train station in Los Angeles. I said good-bye and began the lumbering 1,200-mile journey to Seattle. It was the first time I had ever been away from home. By the second night, I reached Portland, Oregon. The next train did not leave until the following morning, so I found a hotel room for a lonely stay. This was the greatest adventure I'd ever been on in my twenty-one years of life.

The next day, when the train arrived in Seattle, Robbie was there to meet me. He settled me in the Edmond Meany Hotel near the University of

Washington campus and then took me to an office where we could apply for our marriage license. After the three-day required wait, we were married at the University Methodist Church. The young Navy fliers in the newly commissioned Navy flight squadron attended our wedding. It was a sweet ceremony; all that a girl could ever hope for. Robbie had planned it all. The organist was the only other woman at the church. But it was all perfect as far as I was concerned.

We lived at the hotel in a room that looked out over the University of Washington campus. In the distance, we could see snow-capped Mt. Rainier. It was a beautiful place to stay and only cost us five dollars a day. We had dinner every evening at the Sand Point Navy Officers' Club, which was fun for me. It gave me the opportunity to become acquainted with the pilots in the torpedo squadron. They really were such boys! Robbie was one of the oldest, and he was only twenty-four.

We had wonderful weather the month we were in Seattle and the pilots had a chance to fly almost every day. They needed to feel comfortable in that monster 2,000 horse-power new torpedo bomber, which would play such an important role in the war with Japan. I never grew to have any positive feeling about those powerful *Avengers* they flew. To me, the plane always seemed like a huge, ungainly, fire-spitting brute. The pilots loved the bomber, and naturally the wives, though afraid, were proud of their men.

We left Seattle the first week in April, when Navy Flight Squadron VC-7 was transferred to El Centro, California, for bombing and night flight training. Robbie did not have to make the flight, because he got permission to drive us back to California. He owned the most impractical but impressive car one could imagine. It was a 1934 yellow Cadillac convertible, a custom-made wonder that had originally belonged to the famous motion picture actress, Norma Shearer.

We drove to Portland and then over to the beautiful Coast Highway, almost abandoned during the war because of gas rationing. What a fantastic drive it was, all along the Oregon coast and then through the gigantic redwood forests of northern California. There was a rim on the wheel of the car that kept pinching one of the tire tubes. Robbie had to repair the tire thirteen times on the trip! He never lost his temper nor seemed frustrated. This impressed me and I know it set a true direction for our marriage, which has remained steady all of these years.

We stopped over in Long Beach, California, to see our families and then drove on to El Centro. Robbie's squadron, VC-7, was stationed at the Marine Air Base until July 1943. The married couples set up housekeeping at the Barbara Worth Hotel. Our salary, even with flight pay, was so low we did our laundry in the bathtub and ate a lot of grilled cheese sandwiches, prepared on a little hot plate we kept in the hotel room. Our generation was one that would never have considered asking parents for financial help. We found ways to make our money stretch. However, our finances did get lean by the end of each month.

Despite the financial pinch, we had our good times while we were in El Centro. We became friends with the other newly married couples. All the squadron wives had only what we could create for ourselves to fill the long days in the small town. Since I had our Cadillac convertible available, some of us would drive to Calexico once in a while to get gas in Mexico. Other times I would drive them out to the base to meet our husbands for dinner at the Officer's Club. That yellow car was easy to spot on the empty roads. Robbie and the other squadron pilots, when they were out practicing, would love to make low-level torpedo runs on us. The way their motors roared as they dove by in those massive bombers scared us half-to-death. Now, after all these years, I can still remember and feel that thundering vibration, which shook us as they zoomed by. They would pull up at the last moment to clear the trees that lined the fields. The trees were windbreaks to protect the crops.

One night they dove in over the Barbara Worth Hotel shortly after midnight to give us a thrill. The roar of the planes shook the town! The next morning the so-called attack was headlines in the paper. All they did was to wake everyone up. The squadron got into trouble, but the Navy was so in need of torpedo pilots that they let them off with a reprimand. It was forbidden play, but no one was hurt and it did provide a diversion for the pilots of VC-7. It was also excellent practice in the life-and-death low flying they were destined to do.

I shall never forget Easter Sunday, 1943. We had a wonderful day together. All of the pilots were decked out in their white uniforms and the girls were in their pretty 1940 dresses. We decided to top off our perfect day by going for a spaghetti feed in one of El Centro's Main Street restaurants. Before we finished our dinner, a couple of shore patrol officers came in.

"All pilots report immediately to the base!" they ordered. I drove some of the pilots and their wives out to the base. Our skipper, Commander Bill Bartlett, was waiting in the ready room for all of the pilots to arrive. He had received orders that a flight of unidentified planes was approaching the area, and the squadron was to intercept the enemy. We girls said goodbye, watched as they fired up the *Avengers* and took off with a roar into the night, wondering what in the world would happen to our husbands. That was my first brush with the reality of war and how fast the fun of a wonderful day could evaporate. Though this suspected attack turned out to be a false alarm, it was a forerunner of times to come.

By the summer of 1943, we were on our way, again; this time to Coronado, California. The squadron was based at the North Island Naval Air Station across the bay from San Diego. The fighter pilots were reassigned to a new squadron fighting in the Solomon Islands in the South Pacific. One of the fighter pilots to leave with the new Grumman *Hellcat* fighters was our best friend, Pat Patterson. He had gone to the University of Southern California with Robbie.

A few weeks later, the news came. Pat was missing after engaging the enemy in the fight to stop the advance of the Japanese. The last time Pat was seen, a *Zero* fighter was firing on his plane. Pat never returned. It was so hard. Robbie went to see his mother in Hollywood. She always believed Pat would return—but he was gone.

During this time, the torpedo/bombing division of VC-7 was assigned to a secret project. This gave Robbie and me a few more months together. I found out later, Squadron VC-7 was the first squadron to be equipped with air-to-ground rockets. In fact, Robbie was selected as the test pilot to work with the California Institute of Technology, and he fired these first rockets at a secret place near Death Valley. I didn't know at the time all that he was doing. It was done in great secrecy.

Squadron VC-7 was training for a new kind of precision flying, not only in the firing of rockets, but also in night-attack work with use of the first radar equipment. Theirs was the first squadron to go to war with rockets and radar. I missed Robbie terribly during the nights he was gone. For me, it was a dark time of tension and worry.

We rented a room in the home of a marine colonel's wife. It was less than a block from the entrance to the North Island Naval Air Station. This was convenient. Coronado was a delightful little military town, but it was hard to fill the days when the boys were gone.

During this time, I had an ectopic pregnancy. This necessitated an emergency operation at the North Island Naval Hospital. What a physical and emotional blow it was. It took sometime to recover and readjust. I remember the sadness we felt, because we had hoped for a child and now that wasn't to be.

It had been quite a year. We had lived in thirteen different places and our future together was uncertain. Now it was only a matter of time until the squadron would leave to fight the Japanese in some far away place in the Pacific. Soon our husbands would be sent into the unknown of war, for which they had trained so intensively. Life was beyond control! The situation had become unreal, so uncertain and so earnest in a way I had never before experienced. The second day of January, 1944, we said goodbye. The squadron had completed their intensive training, including carrier qualification of their new aircraft carrier, the *USS Manila Bay*, and the pilots were ready to go.

It is difficult to describe the mixture of emotions I felt on the day the carrier left the dock at North Island. There was a hectic inner excitement bordering on hysteria, even as it was necessary to maintain an appearance of calm assurance. As I think about it now, I wonder at the self-control the flyers' wives displayed, as the *Manila Bay* left San Diego. We were all so young.

Once the ship left the dock, was turned by the tugs, and headed down the channel under its own power to the open sea, several of us went to the home of the skipper's wife, Sis Bartlett, to spend a few more moments before saying good-bye. The girls had become close during the months we had spent together. Now we were going our separate ways. In most cases we would never see one another again.

The anxiety I had experienced for so long intensified as I returned to live with my parents in Long Beach. As loving as they were, there was no way they could relate to the loss of those close relationships I had developed in the squadron. There was no one I could talk with about all I had been through during the year of 1943.

The night of February 3, 1944, the doorbell rang at my parents' home. I opened the door. There stood a Western Union Telegram delivery boy. And my world stopped. I knew. . . I just knew. Trembling, I read the words:

WESTERN UNION
WASHINGTON D. C.
MRS JOAN LARRIMER ROBINSON   1944 FEB 3 PM 6 35

We regret to inform you that your husband,
Lieutenant F. W. Robinson has been critically
injured while in combat in the South Pacific.
We will notify you when we receive more
information. Please do not divulge the name
of his ship or station.

REAR ADMIRAL RANDALL JACOBS CHIEF NAVAL PERSONNEL

---

*   *   *

That night I walked the streets of Long Beach with my father. The storm thrashed palm trees and cast the shadows of their sweeping fronds across the wet pavement. The rain washed my cheeks as the tears fell.

Four months passed and I could only live a day at a time. No further information came. Then one day, I received a thoughtful letter from a nurse serving in a naval hospital above Pearl Harbor. She wrote, in part, "Robbie is recovering." I had prayed continually for my husband and my prayers had been answered.

There were months ahead of separation and anxiety before we could put the war behind us and build our lives anew. By the end of 1944, Robbie had healed enough to go on another tour of duty north of New Guinea. Finally, in 1945, victory over Japan came. World War II was over.

After the war we began our family. We built a home in North Hollywood. By this time two of our children had been born, first our daughter Gail, and then our son Franklin Willard III. Robbie had started his new career in education, meeting with continued success as he took the competitive examinations for teaching and administrative positions within the Los Angeles Unified School District.

These were hard and demanding times for both Robbie and me; for I learned my mother was suffering from breast cancer. Out of fear, mother had kept her secret for four years. By the time we learned of the illness, the cancerous growth had progressed so far that we had no alternative but to support her. She had long before made the fatal decision not to seek medical treatment.

Dad, Sister, and I were not involved with Christian Science. But, the only loving thing we felt we could do was to support her. I assumed the responsibility for taking my terminally ill mother, at her persistent request, to a Christian Science practitioner in Glendale. I did this every week, until Mother became too weak to leave her bed. I made this long trip in our 1937 Ford coupe, with our two babies, leaving North Hollywood early in the morning to pick up Mother. It was a long trip to Glendale, then back to Long Beach, and then in the afternoon to North Hollywood. There were no freeways in those days. This was all I could do for my mother.

In November 1950, I got a telephone call from Dad. " I don't think your mother has too much time left," he said. Immediately, I drove to Long Beach. I found my mother in a coma.

"I'm going to call the practitioner," I said to my sister. "Perhaps if he comes and sits by the bed, she'll get some comfort." I quickly dialed his number. Perhaps this was impulsive, but I was driven to do something

151

"I can't come," he said. "I can do as much for her here as I could do if I came."

"But, think how humane it would be if you'd come and tell my mother you love her and pray for her," I pleaded!

"No, I can't do that."

"Then you're no damn good!" I was shaking with anger. "Then you're a fake and a phony! If you cared anything about her, and all the money she's paid you, and the pain she's suffered to travel to you, you'd at least give her the comfort of your presence."

"No, I won't come," he answered dispassionately

I held my mother's hand as she died. She endured all of this – her long battle with cancer – without ever seeing a doctor. Mother was fifty-five years old. It was a family tragedy. At the time I was left with a hurt and bitterness I did not share.

Almost ten years later, in a class at the Bel Air Presbyterian church, it all came out. Dr. Neil Warren, a Clinical Psychologist, was teaching on the subject of death from cancer. In the discussion that followed, someone said, "That's far-fetched. It couldn't be like that. No one dies of cancer that way."

This tripped a repressed load of anger in me. "You don't know what you are talking about!" I actually screamed. I was very emotional and did lose my self control. I didn't understand at the time what was going on with me, but I did realize I needed help. It was then that I talked with Dr. Warren. "Will you take me as a patient? I really need you," I pleaded.

I was in therapy with Dr. Warren for several months. He was Dean of the School of Psychology at Fuller Seminary in Pasadena. My decision to go to Dr. Warren was the hardest and loneliest I had ever made on my own, but it proved to be an important step on my journey to wholeness.

Shortly after my mother's death, we moved further west in the San Fernando Valley to Tarzana, California. I decided we should be involved in a church. After all, isn't that what good families do? And so we joined the St. James Presbyterian Church, which was being organized near our new home.

Somehow, I never felt free to do this while my mother was living. Now I had met this wonderful little Scottish pastor, Calvin Duncan. I responded to his sincerity and love for Christ. I asked him to baptize me. For me to accept Christ at that time was more a decision of the mind than it was a response to the Spirit. This is not exactly true either, but it explains the process, for God was initiating a relationship within my life, which was to continue and grow over the years. My confused religious background didn't help me in making a relationship with the living Christ exceptionally clear. It would take time.

In 1955, Robbie and I, along with our children, Gail and Tri, sailed to Peru, as guests on one of our brother's large iron ore carrier ships. On the return voyage, as we entered the Pacific side of the Panama Canal, the captain received a radio message. My father had died in the Veterans' Hospital in Westwood, California. He had enlisted and been trained as a soldier in World War I.

Dad had been ill for some time. But we were assured before leaving for Peru that his death was not imminent, so this news did come as a shock. We couldn't get home for his funeral!

The truth is, my father was ineffective in many ways and he never did recover from the loss of my mother. I would describe him as a loving, sensitive Irishman who could never get his act together. Basically, he lived in a fantasy world. I know now, it was his way of dealing with failure and loss. The Great Depression hit him hard. He denied the reality of his life. The important thing is, my father did give me a lot of love and I responded to him in a positive way. Both of my parents are buried in the Westminster Cemetery. That's not far off the 405 Freeway, between Santa Ana and Long Beach, California.

*   *   *

Our youngest daughter, Dana Hope, was born in June of 1959. We had waited for her for eleven years and thought we'd never have another child. Gail was thirteen and Tri was eleven when Dana was born. She was a gift; a miracle.

Our joy was overshadowed by a serious infection I contracted immediately following her birth. This necessitated a prolonged thirty-day stay in the hospital, during which time I could not even see my little girl. I remember vividly the day, when a month after the birth, I held Dana in my arms for the first time. I cried with joy! Two years later, because of my poor health, I faced the reality of another major operation: a hysterectomy. I had a serious problem with adhesions as a result of three previous major operations. This would complicate the operation. The afternoon following the surgery, I had a massive internal hemorrhage. My blood pressure was gone. I had no pulse, no heartbeat. Robbie was in the room with me when this happened. He knew something was seriously wrong. I could not speak. "Get in here!" Robbie yelled, as he ran down the hospital corridor for help. A team of medics, including the doctor who was on duty, rushed to the room with a lot of emergency medical apparatus. The hospital attendants attached wires to my prone body.

Robbie told me later that the doctor watched the dials on the machine with great intensity. I couldn't talk while all of this was going on, but I could hear every word being said. In a moment I heard the doctor say, "She's gone." Robbie pleaded with the doctor, "No, don't let her go, keep working." The doctor cut a gash in my leg, just above the ankle, and into my vein they pumped a massive blood transfusion. It was then I began to respond. Another major operation that night saved my life. This may seem strange, but I could hear everything that was going on in the room during this time. When the doctor said, "She's gone," I wanted to scream, "No, I'm not gone! I'm here! Please, please keep working. Help me!" My ears could still hear, when nothing else in my body could respond. Again, I was in for a long recovery.

During these years, Robbie continued with his studies at USC and moved through a number of positions in the Los Angeles Unified School District: Vice Principal at Mark Twain Junior High School in Venice, Vice Principal and Principal of Reseda High School, and Principal of Airport Junior High School in Westchester.

*   *   *

In 1959 Robbie resigned from the Los Angeles Unified School District to become the Principal of Beverly Hills High School. I relate this, because in a way I had a part in the transition. This is how it happened. At the time of his graduation from USC with a doctorate degree in education, Dr. Melbo, Dean of the School of Education, called Robbie and me to his office. I was surprised to be asked by the Dean to attend the conference. Dean Melbo was a very nice man. After greeting us he began, in part:

"I wanted you and Joan to come in, because it is important you extend your vision. You have a future as far as your educational carrier is concerned. When these opportunities come, you need to make the decision together."

I was amazed that he included me in the process. This was very unusual. Dr. Melbo continued, now speaking directly to Robbie:

"I know you feel secure as a principal in Los Angeles, but keep the door open. There is opportunity out there if you have the courage to move, and I want to give you the assurance that USC will be behind you."

This was high praise from the Dean, and it did give us the courage we needed to even consider Robbie ever leaving the security of the Los Angeles City School system.

Later, Dr. Melbo's recommendation opened the door for Robbie to become the Principal of Beverly Hills High School. It was reward to know I had a part in the process.

It was during this time that Calvin Duncan, pastor of our church in Tarzana, left. I decided it might be best for the family to move to the newly organized Bel Air Presbyterian Church, where Don Moomaw was the pastor. I soon became active in their training program for Christian counseling. It was a special time for me.

Ken Working, one of the assistant pastors, served on a committee to establish a new Extension Program for Fuller Seminary. He surprised me, when he asked, "Joan, would you consider the administrative position for Fuller Seminary's pilot program for the Los Angeles area?"

To do this would be a tremendous challenge. I had never taken on an assignment like this in my life. I really wanted to try.

Robbie encouraged me, "You are great for the position. Working with people seeking a dimension of ministry for their lives is an assignment for which you're perfect!"

My office, as Director of the Fuller Seminary Extension Program, was located at the Bel Air Presbyterian Church on Mulholland Drive. From there I could look out over the San Fernando Valley. This was perfect for me, because it was close to home. Too, it was a good place from which to drive to the many churches in the Los Angeles area that I would be visiting to promote the program. I remember one day I drove over three hundred miles in Los Angeles traffic to accomplish these contacts.

Fuller Seminary set up the programs to be taught. My job was to locate the students who wanted to participate in the Extension Program. It was designed for lay people, who were busy in their secular jobs, but desired a Christian spiritual dimension in their work. Robbie was one of our first students. He told me that he learned more about leadership and communication skills in our programs than he did in any of the classes he had taken in educational administration at the University of Southern California.

The students learned communication skills, how to handle conflict in management and, of course took advantage of the excellent classes in Biblical Studies. We did have wonderful students. Some went on to qualify for theological degrees. However, most of our students wanted only to become more effective in their secular work. We held these classes at the Hollywood Presbyterian Church, a wonderful central location for this work.

My job, as I said, was to recruit the students, make contacts with the teachers, as designated by the seminary, record all student records and process their grades.

The program proved to be a wonderful experience, too, for the seminary professors. To be in dialog with these dedicated students, who were already successful in the secular world, brought a new dimension to the student-professor relationship. The professors found they could not only dispense the truth but they were forced to interact with the stellar minds of their mature students.

I found my work not only challenging but invigorating. I attended all the classes taught; which were two each semester. This was important because it enabled me to develop relationships with the professors and the students.

Because of my earlier work with Dr. Neil Warren, who was also Dean of the highly-rated Fuller School of Psychology, we used a number of those professors in our Extension Program. One of the required classes of their ministerial program was participation in a small group healing experience. Robbie and I were asked to be co-leaders in one of these small groups. We were the first lay persons to be assigned this responsibility at Fuller Seminary.

Later, Dr. David Bock asked me to team with him in his professional counseling program. All of this valuable experience was wonderful. I was getting special training, which later proved so valuable as future opportunities in Christian counseling opened for me.

During this same time, Robbie was experiencing added pressure as Principal of Beverly Hills High School. People were frightened with the demonstrations, which were going on in the schools at the height of the Viet Nam War, and Beverly Hills High had become one of the focal points for community and student discontent. Robbie became committed to doing a better job in communicating with the students and staff, using the skills and principles learned in our Extension Program.

Robbie asked me to help him facilitate a small group experience for staff members in the Beverly Hills School District. It proved to be a valuable experience for the group of about twenty people, who chose to participate. We became dedicated to one another, and it gave me insight and a depth of acceptance by school people I had not experienced before. I met with these new friends every two weeks at the close of the school day. What loving and caring people they were, representing a wide spectrum of responsibility from district administration and supervision, to elementary and high school teaching and counseling. We were men and women, black and white, Christian and Jew, administrator and teacher, all learning to be free as persons ministering to each other and growing in our personal lives.

One good friend, through her tears, confessed, "All my life I knew that I, as a Jew, could never be loved by a Christian. I am in such inner turmoil, because I am loved and I don't know how to deal with this in my own life."

156

Everyone at the school, with few exceptions, came to appreciate Robbie as a human being as well as a super administrator. It's hard to put into words, but if you saw what happened in action you'd know there was softness in him that no one but me had known before. To have this facilitating role in Beverly Hills was a highlight experience for me during the seventeen years Robbie was principal of the high school.

*   *   *

One day during the summer of 1975, the phone rang in our Tarzana home. This was not an unusual event. This call, however, would spark a dramatic change which would uproot our lives. Our friend, Bill Cody, the director of Laity Lodge in the Texas Hill Country, was on the phone.

"Howard Butt asked me to call you," he said to Robbie. "Would you consider coming to Texas to head a new project for H. E. Butt and Laity Lodge Foundations? We are looking for a director of lay theological education. You'd work with us and a dozen theological schools in the Southwest."

Robbie and I were well acquainted with Howard Butt's dynamic lay ministry and the support his successful family grocery chain had given to Christian Leadership Conferences across the United States. It was a challenging thought, but Robbie wanted to dismiss it as less than a responsible thing to do. He was at the height of his professional career and holding the position of principal of the high school was still personally rewarding.

I, too, was well-established at the Fuller Theological Seminary as the administrator of their extension program and Dana, our youngest daughter, was in the midst of a happy and successful junior year at Beverly Hills High School. Our heritage in southern California had great depth and we delighted in being with our children. However, I knew Robbie. I thought he was a little abrupt in telling Bill Cody that he was not interested in the job and that he didn't want to move to Texas! Fortunately, Bill Cody ended the conversation by saying, "I know how you feel, but think it over. I'll call you back in two days."

After Robbie hung up the phone, I confronted him. "I heard three things in the conversation, which really bothered me. If we're a partnership, then *Number one*, you didn't include me in the conversation. *Number two*, you said Dana was going to be a junior in high school. If you're going to use Dana as an excuse, you should ask her. She might have her own ideas about this! *Number three*, we haven't prayed."

"Well, you're right," Robbie said. "Would you really consider living in Texas?" I told him, I didn't say I was closed to the idea. I'm saying that we should be open to that possibility. I really felt this was a family decision, and for all I knew, this might open a whole new ministry opportunity for us. At least we should talk with Howard Butt.

Later we asked Dana how she would feel about a possible move. "I've never lived in a small town. This would be my only opportunity to have this experience. I'm so lucky to be here. Since I was born so late in your lives, what you do shouldn't be controlled by me. You need to do what is best for you and I will adjust. I'll be off to college in a couple of years anyway."

As I talked with Robbie, I told him he should consider that in a couple of years he would be at his maximum retirement benefits at Beverly Hills High. Robbie was not ready to retire. I knew him. He would always need a challenge and a cause. I told him we should at least go to Kerrville, Texas, and meet with Howard Butt. That made sense to Robbie. He agreed it was the sensible thing to do.

Bill Cody called back two days later. He was the director of Laity Lodge and the spokesman for Howard Butt. We were prepared to give him an answer.

"We'll come to Texas to talk with you and Howard," Robbie said. "That is all I can say. But if Joan and I come, there is something you will need to consider. I can't come just for another job. If we come it will have to be on the basis of a joint ministry that includes Joan. Howard Butt might have a problem with this, so let me know."

Robbie felt strongly about my involvement. He respected my experience in building educational programs for the laity, and felt that it would be unfair to tear me from my position in the Fuller Seminary Extension Program without some continued participation for me in Christian work.

Arrangements were made and Robbie and I boarded a Continental Airlines flight to Texas, landed in San Antonio and drove west for sixty miles over Interstate 10. The rolling hill country slipped by as we moved easily over the green ridges covered with cedar and Spanish oak, past the valleys of the Guadalupe River, and through the limestone bluffs and aquifers laid down in some prehistoric sea.

It was shortly after the noon hour when we dropped over the last ridge and entered Kerrville, Texas, location of the H.E. Butt Foundation. What a picturesque and peaceful setting it was. There were two identical English stone cottages shaded by large pecans, a giant oak and a magnificent magnolia tree. Howard Butt was waiting for us in his spacious, paneled office, furnished tastefully with antique furniture and comfortable couches.

"So glad you could come," he greeted us. We met his wife, Barbara Dan, and the rest of the staff. For the better part of the next two days, we talked.

Naturally, we needed clarification on the organization of the foundations and specific expectations of our proposed work.

"We have three foundations;" Howard explained, "the H.E. Butt Foundation, the Laity Lodge Foundation and Christian Men Incorporated. Your work would be within the Laity Lodge and Christian Men Foundations. Both are designed to bring quality educational programs to the laity. You would be responsible for some retreat work at Laity Lodge, sixty miles west of here on two-thousand acres along the Frio River. But primarily you would be developing a new program, a joint project between our foundation and twelve seminaries in the Southwest. We are anxious to bring the resources of the seminaries to areas throughout the country and provide a program of continuing education for the laity."

Howard Butt had a vision for the laity. It was a vision to which we could respond.

"We have generated an age of specialization and professionalism," he explained, "and advertently, or inadvertently, abdicated our spiritual role in the world to a professional clergy not always prepared to minister in the earthy relationships of the market place. Lay ministry is naturally ecumenical. We don't work in Baptist labor unions. Those in public education don't teach in Methodist institutions, nor do we live on Catholic streets or buy in Presbyterian stores."

Howard was getting wound up by this time. Robbie and I loved his enthusiasm; his intensity.

"The ecumenical nature of the lay ministry is not always accepted by the established church hierarchy. The conflict you have gone through in the secular world is nothing compared to what you will experience as you begin to work with mature and professional Christians."

"You mean the battle over the Bible?" Robbie asked.

"No, that can be a front. I see it more as an attempt to protect the *status quo*, by both the lay and professional leadership, to hold tight to their power in the Christian world."

"You make it sound pretty formidable," I said.

Howard continued, "Robbie could make a contribution as the director of this program with the seminaries. He knows administration and could build creative educational models for us. I know that! He would not be a threat, either, working with these mature and professional Christian people."

Robbie then approached the question of our working together in building these programs. I had been actively involved in the discussion and fortunately it had become apparent to the staff that I would bring an added dimension to the ministry. It was settled. Robbie and I could work together!

Then it became clear that we needed to respond to this call. Aspects of the mission were still frightening to me. There was so much ambiguity. We would be starting from scratch, but it was a challenge, and God had prepared Robbie and me for this dynamic leadership training.

*   *   *

The pain I felt in saying farewell to family and friends was congruent with the flow of my life, as it moved toward a destiny I could accept only on faith. In a way I was experiencing a death, and with it the crucifixion of so much that was of value in my life. The faithfulness to the sovereignty of Christ no longer was an intellectual exercise. I wept when the moving van, with all our belongings, rolled down the hill toward Texas. I was left in an empty home that I loved. However, not even then did I question our decision.

On January 1, 1976, we were on Interstate Highway 10, driving east between the Rio Grande and Pecos Rivers in route to our new home in Kerrville, Texas. The early morning sky began to lighten. It was cold. Wisps of snow blew in traces across the highway as we drove over the mountain pass to Van Horn, Texas.

"I can't believe we are doing this," I said. "It all seems like a dream. This is unreal!"

I was thinking, too, about our sixteen-year-old daughter who was half-asleep on the back seat. Dana had not stood in the way of our decision and that had solidified her as a member of the family team on this adventure.

In a few moments I broke the silence, "I brought a tape of the sermon Howard Childers preached at Bel Air. Do you remember it? It's 'The Day the Wind Hit the Sails.' We need to hear it again." I slipped the tape into the panel below the dashboard.

Howard had been the Associate Pastor at the Bel Air Presbyterian Church in the hills above Los Angeles. He was a talented and relational Texas A&M graduate who organized the small group ministry in our church. In a moment his familiar and warm Texas drawl came alive as we sped along.

This morning I'm going to talk with you about Pentecost. That was the day the wind hit the sails and it changed the world. This never would have happened if those inadequate, frightened and confused people, in the doldrums of their lives, had not, in obedience and faithfulness hoisted their listless sails. God filled their sails and they moved out in a new power under the unction of the Spirit to bring healing to a waiting world.   *(Howard Childers)*

I reached over and put my hand on Robbie's arm. Then the gray Texas sky eased into a sunrise of gold, and with the new day came again "the assurance of what we hoped for and the certainty of what we did not yet see." (Hebrews 11:1)

In January 1976, we arrived at an apartment we had already rented in Kerrville, Texas. All of our belongings from California – boxes, crates and furniture – had been jammed into the small area we were to temporarily call home. What a mess! I didn't know where to start.

Fortunately, a couple of new friends from the Foundation came and worked with us to open boxes, sort out furniture that needed to be stored, and to arrange the small kitchen. By evening we did have places to sleep and the ability to cook a meal. We had arrived.

By the end of the month, we had purchased adjoining lots at the new Riverhill Country Club in Kerrville. It was a wonderful place where Robbie and I could play golf. Our new home would be built in a beautiful location on the edge of a lake in the center of the golf course. We decided that if we built a duplex, rather than a single-family dwelling, we could sell one of them for enough to have the other half of the duplex free and clear of any debt. It did work out that way. I was so happy with our new home.

Our new home had fifty-four Pella windows, which captured the views of the lake. From our bed in the master bedroom, we could look out over the lake and see the sunrise. Around two oak trees, we built two secluded atriums within the structure of the house for hanging baskets. From other windows we could see the greens and fairways of the golf course. We heard it was said, "That house is being built by some crazy people from California." However, when the other half of our duplex was purchased, for the full price, by the Publisher of the Dallas Times Herald, that put a stop to the "crazy talk."

Our offices were in one of the stone cottages on Foundation property. Soon Robbie was assigned the responsibility of redesigning the place into office space for our work. This was good for me, because they took out the kitchen and built a beautiful little office for me. It was right next to Robbie's office and we had a secretary.

Now, in a few short months, I had an office, a beautiful home, and a new 1975 Toyota. We joined the Kerrville First Presbyterian Church and I was elected a church elder. Our pastor, Neil Wheatherhog, asked me to help him with his sermons. I found this a rewarding assignment.

Dana finished her junior year at Tivy High School with a straight A academic record. However, they would not let her join the Honor Society, even though she had brought a perfect record from Beverly Hills High School.

Robbie talked with the principal of the high school and found they had a rule that a student had to be in the school for two years before qualifying for honors.

"Forget it," Robbie told Dana. "With your record, you can get into Schrinier College, right here in Kerrville. I'll call Beverly Hills High School and tell them to send you a high school diploma now." And they did. This was a good move, because a year later all of Dana's Shrinier credits were accepted by Texas A&M in College Station, Texas, where she received her B.A. and Masters Degree in Psychology. Dana was an exceptional student.

The part of my job with the foundation which I most enjoyed was the relationships I developed with key professors in the thirteen seminaries. All of these educational institutions belonged to the Council of Southwest Theological Schools. The professors we worked with, in organizing the lay projects throughout the Southwest, became very special new friends.

This was the way the projects were usually organized. Robbie and I would meet with a selected committee in an interested church. Meeting with these leaders, we would assess their requests and help them organize an educational program to meet their desires. This meant suggesting and setting up courses of study, recommending the teachers, and setting dates, times and places for the teaching seminars. My specific responsibility was to coordinate the planning that went into a successful event. We met many wonderful people during the seven years we worked with the churches and seminaries.

If there was a drawback to our job, it would be the many times we were away from our home in Kerrville. Texas and the Southwest is a vast territory. Robbie and I drove many miles. The teaching projects ranged from as far east as Lufkin, Texas, and west to Los Alamos, New Mexico, a distance of a thousand miles. It ranged from Tulsa, Oklahoma, in the north, to Brownsville, Texas on the Mexico border in the south. That was another thousand miles. On these trips, as we dropped over the last hills on our return to Kerrville, I remember always saying, "Robbie, I can't believe we live in Kerrville, Texas!" Somehow, it seemed unreal.

There were fun times, too. Riverhill was a wonderful place to play golf. Robbie and I were both playing well. We loved to participate in the weekly "scrambles." This was a couples tournament, and they always liked to have me on their teams, because I was a good putter. Putting is usually where the tournament is won or lost. How, now, I wish I could play again.

I learned to play tennis, too. Dorothy Parish, Howard Butt's secretary, was married to Henry Parish, the tennis pro at Riverhill. Henry always wanted Dorothy to play tennis, but she had been reluctant. Because Robbie and I were beginners, she agreed to play doubles, and Henry could be her partner. It was a great arrangement. We played night after night, learning from one of the great pros in the country. We always had a wonderful time, because Henry knew how to place his shots, so we all had a chance to keep in the game. What a talented and loving man Henry Parish was. We cherished our friendship.

Robbie had always been a runner. It was his way of keeping in shape and dealing with frustration and stress. I had started to do this while we were still living in Tarzana, California, and continued to run early in the morning on the beautiful Riverhill fairways. This was another activity Robbie and I enjoyed together. It was great fun and I ran very well. In 1980, I won first place in the six-mile Kerrville River Run in the 50-year-and-older division. Later, I entered the Capitol 10,000 Meter Run (six miles) in Austin, Texas. There were 26,000 runners in the race and I won a beautiful trophy by finishing in second place, Female Masters, March 19, 1984.

*   *   *

We found our responsibilities, while working for the H.E. Butt Foundation, were flexible, diverse, interesting, challenging and sometimes frustrating. Robbie and I were on call seven days a week, if needed. Too, there were often periods of time where there was little direction. This could be frustrating, especially for Robbie, a super-organized administrator in his former professional life.

Shortly after our arrival at the H. E. Butt Foundation, Robbie and I were assigned, with others, as conveners for the North American Congress of the Laity, to be held in Los Angeles. This was a tremendous and costly undertaking, which entailed extensive travel and time away from Kerrville. President Gerald Ford was the Honorary Chairman. I could throw out a lot of names of world leaders who were in attendance. One of my fondest memories is of the month we spent hosting Malcomb and Kitty Muggeridge in the Laguna Beach (California) home of Ted and Bobbie Robinson. Malcolm was finishing the last of his five-volume memoir, The Wasted Years. We would laugh and say, "Malcolm, you sure wasted a lot of time before you became a Christian!" What a gift to walk the beaches of Laguna with the Muggeridges. They were so very English: stodgy, opinionated, humorous, and fun. It was a memorable time.

*   *   *

An added bonus, during the time we were in Kerrville, was our continued involvement at Laity Lodge on the Frio River in the Texas Hill County. On occasion, during the time when there would be a change in directors, we led retreats. Other times we were asked to be at Laity Lodge as support personnel.

163

We had a beautiful apartment, a short distance from the Lodge, which cantilevered over the lake from Black Bluff. Primarily our responsibility was to relate to the guests—and they still called it work. However, Robbie was asked to take over the supervision of some of the remodeling and the installation of air conditioning for the guest apartments. Robbie especially enjoyed this assignment.

One of my fondest memories of Laity Lodge came through the generosity of Barbara Dan and Howard Butt. Dana was married in the Great Hall. To celebrate the occasion, our family and friends came from as far away as California and New Mexico for the three day reunion. What fun we had!

To have Laity Lodge all to us as a family was such a blessing. I still remember the wonderful food, swimming in the clear water of the Frio River, the boisterous tennis matches, the young people taking the high dive from the rock ledge into the Black Hole of the river, and the canoe races. We were blessed.

By the end of 1982, Robbie and I decided our work with the Council of Southwestern Theological Schools, the H. E. Butt Foundation and Laity Lodge was winding down. I knew him. Robbie needed a new challenge.

In early 1983 Robbie was asked by Gary Dennis, pastor of the large Westlake Hills Presbyterian Church in Austin, Texas, to become their Minister of Education. I had known Gary when he was a student at Fuller Seminary. We had also led retreats for the Westlake Church at Laity Lodge, so we did know a number of the members of the church. Robbie agreed to go to Austin for a three-year time to build an educational program for their new and growing church. It was a challenging undertaking, because he would be in charge of all the administration of Christian education from the nursery through adult programs. Robbie asked me to take over the responsibility of the adult education, which included special seminars and retreats, much of what I had been doing. We immediately sold our beautiful home at Riverhill and moved to a small one-bedroom apartment in Austin. Even before the move was completed, we bought a town house lot near the Austin Country Club and began the construction of a new home on Fawn Creek.

The three years in Austin were difficult for us. Although we made a number of wonderful friends, I did come down with a serious bout of pneumonia and a delayed recovery. We became disillusioned with the leadership of the church and this put added stress on Robbie, who, in spite of it all, led a number of dedicated people into building an exemplary educational program for the church.

While we were in Austin a recession hit the building boom that Austin had experienced, and our new home took over a year to build because of contractor problems. However, by 1985, we were in our new home: a beautiful secluded place on Fawn Creek. From our bedroom we could hear the water cascade over the rocks.

In early April, 1986, I flew to California to spend time with our children, Tri and Nancy, and our baby grandchildren on the old Robinson Canyon Ranch. I stayed in the "Eagle's Nest," a shed we had converted into a one-room cabin, with a tiny kitchen and a bath. A single pine cone, thrown into the pot-belly stove fire, made it a cozy place. The view out the window from my bed was through the pines to the giant oaks of the valley, over the red hills and on to the Tehachapi Mountains, the sweeping arm of the High Sierras. I was nostalgic. It brought back many memories. With all its harshness, there was a peace here.

I returned to Austin on Easter weekend, 1986. Robbie was at the airport to meet me. "I had a special time at the ranch," I said. "I really think I could live there for a while." That was enough for Robbie. He resigned as Minister of Education at the Westlake Presbyterian Church on the Monday morning after Easter. The next decade of our life was about to begin.

*   *   *

The years at Robinson Canyon Ranch were bittersweet for me. The first year we lived in the Eagle's Nest, a one-room shed cabin without electricity, while we built a new home on the west side of Robinson Canyon. What a major project the building of our new home became! Dealing with Los Angeles County was difficult! Robbie worked so hard to resolve all the problems: a canyon flood plain, the San Andreas earthquake fault, bringing in power and phone service, a defaulting builder who could not finish the job, endless inspections, an unstable building site (Robbie built massive rock walls to stabilize it), and the massive snow falls that kept us from the work site. Hardest of all was when Robbie had bypass heart surgery in San Diego. I had a bout of pneumonia, and I also learned that I would eventually lose my eyesight due to macular degeneration.

Then, in 1990, Tri, Nancy and our grandchildren, Kate and Brook, left the old ranch to start a new Vineyard Church in Boise, Idaho. We waved as they drove off in their old trucks and trailers, loaded with their belongings. A part of my life went with them.

There were wonderful years at the Robinson Canyon Ranch, too. Robbie and I, for the first time, shared our independent life. It was a life that was isolated, in a spectacular California setting, but at times there was a special peace, too. Robbie was happy. I loved working in my flower gardens, taking my runs through the valleys of blooming sage and majestic oaks, and entertaining friends in our beautiful new home. We drove fifty miles each Sunday to attend church at the Desert Vineyard, in Lancaster, and became involved in church activities.

In 1987 Robbie and I went to Auckland, New Zealand, with John Wimber, as members of his ministry team. What an amazing and growing experience this was. Three years later we returned to New Zealand to teach in the South Pacific School of Missions. We also taught, on occasion, at the International School of Missions that our pastor son, Tri, had started at our old Corona del Valle Ranch. Over the years, hundreds of students attended this school, from all over the world.

We were asked to teach evening classes in homiletics and Christian counseling to prospective church leaders at the Desert Vineyard Church. Over the years we facilitated and taught a discipleship home group in our ranch home. These new friends came for miles from Lancaster, Palmdale, Elisabeth and Hughes Lakes, and the west end of the Antelope Valley, for Christian fellowship, learning, sharing, and growth. This was another wonderful experience; a needed opportunity to be with people who were growing in their Christian faith.

The year 1991 began major changes in my life. We had little rain or snow. In January, wind-driven clouds of dust rolled through the west end of the Antelope Valley. Then the rains came. By April, the previously arid desert burst into brilliant color. We hiked the wild-flower-carpeted hills of the Tahachapis with our children, Gail and Steve Van Camp. Our cardiologist son, Steve, said, "Dad you work so hard here on the ranch and hike all over these mountains. I think it would be a good idea to have a stress test."

"Why?" Robbie said. "I feel fine."

On our next trip to San Diego, Robbie did go to Steve's office for an examination. The tests indicated serious artery closure, which could only be solved by triple bypass heart surgery.

Shortly after Robbie's successful surgery, I made up my mind! No way could I live on the ranch, even for a day, if Robbie were not there. It was just too complicated! I remember the time. We were in bed looking out over the red hills and on to the desert, as the rising sun began to light the slopes of the far mountains,

"Robbie," I said, "It's time for us to think about selling the ranch and moving to Boise, Idaho. Tri and Nancy and our grandchildren are there. We could be involved in the church and we wouldn't be so isolated. Neither one of us could live on the ranch alone. We need to make the change while we can."

Robbie was silent. In a moment he said, "Do you realize how complicated it would be to sell the ranch and move to Boise?"

*   *   *

We made several trips to Boise in the next couple of years. Sometimes we drove and other times we flew in a Cessna Skymaster, available for our use. We bought a townhouse in the Pines at River Run, a beautiful new development that was a short walk from the Boise River and the nature trails. It was the perfect place for us, near medical, banking and shopping facilities. Boise State University, the vibrant downtown, the State Capitol, and the Veteran's Hospital were near.

Robbie had been right. The ranch was a complicated property to sell. There were five houses, two gravity-flow springs, several miles of fencing, a well, and extensive lawn and planted areas to maintain. Most difficult of all was the legal ownership of the property itself. Not even the title company, at first, could straighten it out.

Robbie worked on these problems for several months. Some of the original buildings had to be grandfathered in, because they did not have valid permits. There were three parcels of property involved, each one of which had been quitclaimed and deeded back and forth several times since the 1883 homestead had been granted to Harold Sandberg. This went back to President Cleveland's administration in 1883.

Eventually Robbie was able to clear and get Certificate of Compliances on each parcel of property involved in the sale. By the time all of these problems had been worked out, we did have a sale. The property was in escrow in May, 1996, and we made the move to our new home: The Pines at River Run in Boise, Idaho.

*   *   *

As I think today, I look back over the eleven years Robbie and I have lived in Boise. He asked me, "What are your outstanding memories?"

"I don't know," I replied, and then I thought some more. By and large they have been good years. Establishing a new life in Idaho was a timely move. I am comfortable in our home and through the Vineyard church and our discipleship group, I have a number of wonderful friends.

Too, having a son as my pastor has been special. I have watched the church grow into a large and great church. Most important, it is not a great church because it is large; it is large because it is a great church. I am grateful that I have lived to see Tri grow and mature in his gifted ministry.

167

I miss my daughters and my grandchildren. They live in three different states, but with phones and modern travel, we are able to stay in contact. I cherish our visits when they come to Boise, and we now try to fly to Colorado and southern California at least once each year.

The Apostle Paul wrote about the "thorn in his flesh." I have also had to deal with my own thorns. The hardest has been the loss of my eyesight and, with it, my ability to drive. Losing the freedom to independently come and go, without having to depend on others, has been difficult. I have also experienced the challenge of recovering from a major stroke and the loss of some memory. Two knee replacements have been difficult, but now once again, I walk the nature trail along the Boise River. There is life and a peace.

*   *   *

Now, after sixty-four years of marriage, Robbie and I look back on a rich and eventful life; a life full of blessings beyond our greatest dreams. The challenges we have faced over the years have been formative. It is possible to say that the events, both bad and good, have permanently molded our souls and our character. Even the bad times helped in putting us on a path of faith and courage, which has sustained us to this day. We have been blessed.

PARENTS OF JOAN LARRIMER ROBINSON

Ethel Beckwith, Age 19

Born October 5, 1894,
  Anderson, Indiana.
Married 1916,
  Anderson, Indiana.
Died November, 1950,
  Long Beach, California.

Lee Larrimer, Age 26

Born September 22, 1987,
  Warren County, Indiana.
Married 1916,
  Anderson, Indiana.
Died August 1956,
Westwood, California.

Both parents are buried in Westminster Cemetery, Westminister, California.

GENEALOGY OF
JOAN LARRIMER ROBINSON

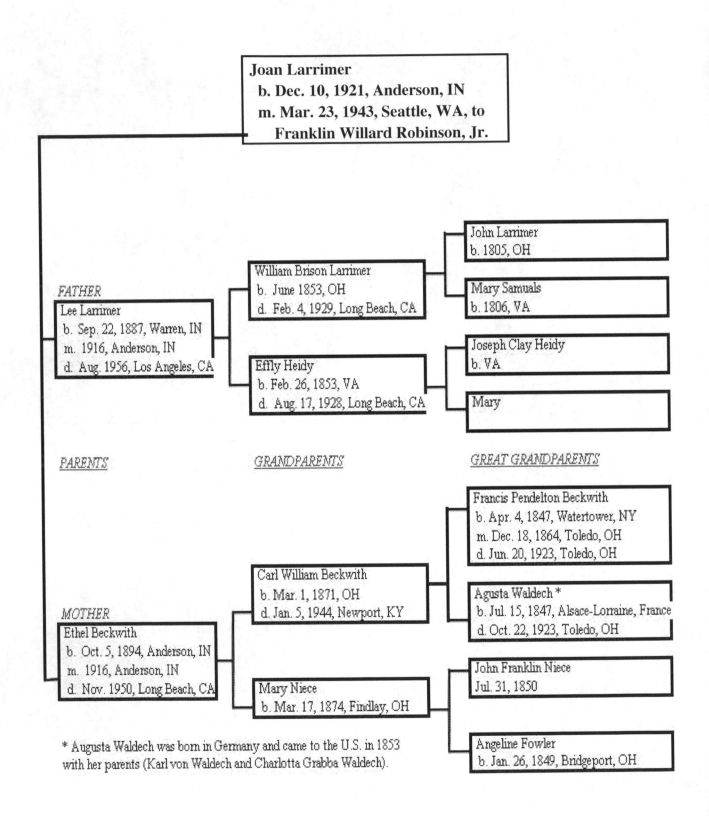

Joan Larrimer
b. Dec. 10, 1921, Anderson, IN
m. Mar. 23, 1943, Seattle, WA, to
Franklin Willard Robinson, Jr.

FATHER
Lee Larrimer
b. Sep. 22, 1887, Warren, IN
m. 1916, Anderson, IN
d. Aug. 1956, Los Angeles, CA

William Brison Larrimer
b. June 1853, OH
d. Feb. 4, 1929, Long Beach, CA

Effly Heidy
b. Feb. 26, 1853, VA
d. Aug. 17, 1928, Long Beach, CA

John Larrimer
b. 1805, OH

Mary Samuals
b. 1806, VA

Joseph Clay Heidy
b. VA

Mary

PARENTS   *GRANDPARENTS*   *GREAT GRANDPARENTS*

Francis Pendelton Beckwith
b. Apr. 4, 1847, Watertower, NY
m. Dec. 18, 1864, Toledo, OH
d. Jun. 20, 1923, Toledo, OH

Carl William Beckwith
b. Mar. 1, 1871, OH
d. Jan. 5, 1944, Newport, KY

Agusta Waldech *
b. Jul. 15, 1847, Alsace-Lorraine, France
d. Oct. 22, 1923, Toledo, OH

MOTHER
Ethel Beckwith
b. Oct. 5, 1894, Anderson, IN
m. 1916, Anderson, IN
d. Nov. 1950, Long Beach, CA

Mary Niece
b. Mar. 17, 1874, Findlay, OH

John Franklin Niece
Jul. 31, 1850

Angeline Fowler
b. Jan. 26, 1849, Bridgeport, OH

* Augusta Waldech was born in Germany and came to the U.S. in 1853
with her parents (Karl von Waldech and Charlotta Grabba Waldech).

170

JOAN LARRIMER AS A BABY GIRL

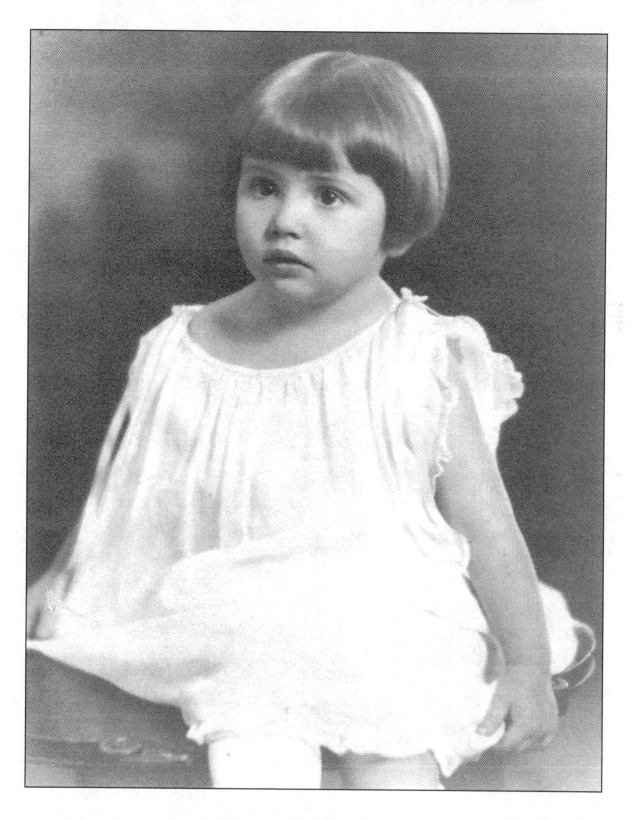

JOAN LARRIMER 1931

Joan Practicing Cello

CHEERLEADER JOAN LARRIMER

**Joan is front left in this 1937 picture
of Long Beach Polytechnical's cheerleaders**

RANCHO CORONA DEL VALLE
October 6, 1938 – Robbie and Joan

Willard Robinson, age 19, and Joan Larrimer, age 15, (five years prior to marriage)

This was Joan's first trip to the Robinson Ranch. Over the years it would become a center around which much of their life would revolve.

The little roan horse in the background was called "Utah." Robbie captured the colt on Wild Horse Mesa in Utah and named it after this state with an abundance of red rock formations.

After breaking Utah in Boulder, Utah, Robbie loaded him up with all his belongings, as a pack horse, and rode "Moki," his black horse, back to the Robinson Ranch in California. Moki was named after the early American Indian tribe that once populated those vast canyon lands, now designated as the Escalante National Monument.

JOAN LARRIMER ROBINSON, MARCH 4, 1945

Long Beach Press Telegram:

"Romance was culminated in wedding vows exchanged by Miss Lee Larrimer, daughter of Mr. And Mrs. Lee Larrimer of this city, and Ensign Franklin Willard Robinson, Jr., United States Naval Air Corps, son of Mr. And Mrs. Franklin Robinson, in the University of Washington Methodist Church. Dr. James Kenna officiated in presence of 30 guests, all members of Ensign Robinson's newly-commissioned Aircraft Carrier Squadron, Torpedo 7.

The former Miss Larrimer, who was at one time a vivacious song leader at Long Beach High School, chose a blue-grey dressmaker suit with matching hat and black accessories for her bridal attire. She carried a small bouquet of orchards, freesias and lilies of the valley. Mrs. Robinson attended Long Beach City College, where she was a member of Tjene Piger, Mahabharata and Socii.

The groom, Ensign Robinson, is temporarily stationed at the Sand Point Naval Air Station, flying the new TBF Grumman Avenger torpedo bomber."

JOAN ROBINSON FAMILY 1949

**Tri, Joan, Gail and Willard Robinson III
1949 in their North Hollywood home**

JOAN LARRIMER ROBINSON
Parachute Jumps – Taft, California
1966

Joan parachutes precisely into the Target area at Taft, California.

Joan has never been too old for adventure!

JOAN ROBINSON
2nd Place Masters Division at Age 63

Capitol 10,000 Meter Run
Austin Texas, 1983

I started running while we were still living in Tarzan, California. I continued running, after we moved to Kerrville, Texas on the beautiful fairways of the the Riverhill Country Club, where we lived. It was great fun and I ran very well. In 1980, I won first place in the six-mile Kerrville River Run in the 50-year and older division. Later, I entered the Capitol 10,000 Meter Run in Austin, Texas. There were 26,000 runners in the race and I won a beautiful trophy.
Joan Robinsons

JOAN ROBINSON'S IMMEDIATE FAMILY

On the Occasion of Joan & Robbie's 50th Anniversary

**Photo taken in 1993 at Warner Hot Springs, California
From left to right: Gail Robinson VanCamp, Tri
Robinson, Joan, husband Robbie and Dana Robinson**

F. WILLARD AND JOAN L. ROBINSON
1998

At the last official reunion of VC-31 and VC-7

This picture of Robbie and Joan Robinson was taken September 1998 in San Diego, California, on the occasion of the last official reunion of World War II Navy Flight Squadrons VC-31 and VC-7. Robbie's Squadron VC-31 was commissioned 55 years before at the Sand Point Naval Air Station in Seattle, Washington, January of 1943.

JOAN IN IDAHO WHITEWATER

August 2005

Joan Robinson (center, closest) at age 83. She is the oldest woman to raft the gorge of the S. Fork of the Payette River from Garden Valley to Banks, in the whitewater capital of the world.

EPILOGUE

There has been great reward in learning about the lives of the ancestors. I share their stories with pride, amazement, and admiration. We live because they lived and loved and persevered.

As a family, now living out our own years, we carry the genes of these courageous forbearers within us. With this knowledge and understanding, our own lives take on added meaning. We now bear the yoke. We carry and pass on, the very being of the past generations. This truth became clearer to me, as I discovered the same ancestral traits within us--the drives, the weaknesses, and the passions, exemplified in those whose stories are told.   In a sense, this is another important dimension of eternal life.

The writing of the Burnett/Kennedy lines of the Robinson Family History began twenty-nine years ago. Now, as I put down my pen, we are in the seventh year of a new century. I am 89 years old.

In 1996, Joan and I sold our portion of the Corona del Valley Ranch, which overlooked the west end of the Antelope valley in Los Angeles County. It was here where, at one time or another, five generations of Robinsons had once lived. There was a wrench in our hearts. But this was the time to move on and establish a new life in Boise, Idaho.

Now, on occasion, I walk the nature trail along the banks of the Boise River. I listen to the movement of the water, as it has for centuries rolled along the river rock. I watch the Canada Geese foil their wings and drop with grace through the cottonwoods to the sanctuaries below. There is awe. Life is a gift and a great mystery. I lift my hands in wonder and thanksgiving for the assured hope of eternal adventure.

Now, too, I give thanks for the gift of faith, which was so ingrained in the very being of these pioneering ancestors. Researching their stories and discovering who they were, I can attest with some assurance that this scripture would be a part of their loving message.

Seek you first the kingdom of God, and all good things will be added unto you.   Matthew 6:33

"Get your priorities right!" they would tell us. This is a valued message for those of us caught in the current conflict between of the values of the secular world, and those of our inherited spiritual foundations. May our Lord continue to bless and keep us.

F. Willard Robinson, 2007

INTRODUCTION TO APPENDIX

As Volume II of <u>The History of the Robinson</u> neared completion, my wife, Joan Robinson, said, " It is important for you to include your own story." I was reluctant to do this, because much of the history was already recorded in my books, <u>Beverly Hills Principal</u>, Writers Press, 1999, and <u>Navy Wings of Gold</u>, River Park Press, 2004.

There was a compromise. In this Appendix, selected pictures and documents, pertaining to my life are included. They are presented with gratitude for the eighty-nine years I have been blessed.

F. Willard "Robbie" Robinson
2007

APPENDIX

LONG BEACH PRESS--TELEGRAM
2,500 Mile Bicycle Journey Finished by Youth

(Editors Note — pedaling home from Michigan, Willard Robinson, bicyclist extraordinary, paused en route to describe his adventures for Press-Telegram readers.)

Home at last, and what a thrill it was to see these old oil derricks on Signal Hill loom on the horizon. Yes, I think I would take the entire trip again just for the thrill of getting home. Although I was only on the road for fourteen and half days it seemed like years. However, the adventure was priceless. I have had the experience of my life.

A little over two weeks ago I gathered together a few clothes and a blanket to start the trip home. I tied my few belongings on the back of the bike and started pedaling down the tree-lined lanes of the lake country near the college town of Ann Arbor, Michigan. I was bound for Long Beach, California.

The first day was one of the hardest on the entire trip. The terrain was level, but I made only a hundred miles. As I dismounted the bike at the end of the day, my legs would hardly hold me. My throat was dry and I felt like I had straddled a pole all day. I was weak from a blood transfusion, which I had given at the Ann Arbor hospital to get the twenty-five dollars I needed for food on the trip. The reality was, I had not had a bicycle to train for the endurance needed for such an adventure. Three days before the start, the English Raleigh Bicycle Company agreed to give me the bike as an advertising gimmick to introduce their new 3-speed geared bike to America.

It was difficult to sleep the first night. There I was, rolled up in a blanket along a Michigan road and so tired I could not sleep. There was no alternative but to keep going. By the third day I reached the Mississippi River, so tired my legs would hardly hold me. But with each following day I would reach my goal at night with more ease and in faster time. In fairly level country I could average twenty-miles-an-hour. In fact, one day across Nebraska, I pedaled 210 miles in fifteen hours.

By the end of the first week, I was in Cheyenne, Wyoming, and feeling stronger each day. It was not too soon, for the next morning I had to climb the 8,000 foot pass of the Rocky Mountains between Cheyenne and Laramie, Wyoming. It was not the hardest part of the day. It hailed as I crossed the pass and rained all the way to Rock Springs. The following night the storm was followed by a cold wind-blown front. I lay in my blanket behind an outhouse for shelter and rest. Today this place is Little America, a valued stop for those traveling across this bleak Wyoming plain.

The vast Nevada desert was the final challenge. There the temperature reached 110 degrees at Baker, the entrance to Death Valley.

A day-and-a-half later I was home. The adventure of my life was behind me. I had averaged 160 miles a day for fourteen-and-a-half straight days in all kinds of weather and terrain. Now I bask in the cool ocean breezes of Long Beach. I am home.

LONG BEACH PRESS-TELEGRAM
August 1937

LONG BEACH PRESS-TELEGRAM

Bicycle Tourist Home

Willard Robinson, home from a 2500-mile bicycle jaunt, smilingly calls the trip the greatest experience of his life.

—Press-Telegram Photo.

LONG BEACH PRESS-TELEGRAM (July 2, 1938)
"Young Adventurers Reach the Escalante"

"Written on a soiled brown paper sack, a letter was received by the Press-Telegram telling of the progress of two Long Beach Polytechnic high school graduates. Willard Robinson and James Dyer are spending the summer exploring a little-known region of the United States, identified as the Escalante Escarpment. The purpose of the trip is to examine the geological and animal life of this canyon-torn area, with hope of finding relics left by the Moki Indians, who centuries ago lived in the canyon cliffs of this remote and seldom explored area.

"Early June 13, the young explorers mounted their bicycles and began the long arduous journey to the uninhabited southeastern regions of Utah. Uneventful was their journey until they crossed the Nevada state line. At that point a blown tire and a thrown chain forced them to push their cycles 42 miles, in over 100-degree-heat, to Las Vegas for repair. On they peddled over two mountain passes of over 9,000 feet and through a land of beautiful lakes and mountains. Eventually the adventurers reached the threshold of their goal. Below stretched 1.7 million acres of what could well be one the world's most dramatic and little-explored natural wonders: the Escalante River and the canyons it has created."

*　　　　*　　　　*

The above article did not report the details of the following month. We arrived in the little town of Escalante, Utah, where we left our bikes, loaded our packs and, against the advice of the "old-timers," began our hike down the gorge of the Escalante River. For much of the way, there were sand bars along river. When the river ran full to the canyon walls, we sought shallow water to make our way. The shear walls of red sandstone towered above us. We found massive amphitheaters, carved over the centuries by the flowing water in which to make our nightly camps. In a sense, we were prisoners within the impenetrable walls of the canyon. Several days later, we sought our way out by turning back up a tributary canyon we thought would eventually take us to little Mormon settlement of Boulder, Utah. Six days later, and now out of food, the canyon narrowed and ahead a sheer wall of cascading water blocked our way. Fortunately, the next day, we began our hike back to the Escalante River. A deer appeared from a patch of willows. With the help of a 22-caliber rifle, we had food at last. Jim and I cut the venison into strips and strung it on a line to dry. In three days we had jerky enough to last us for the rest of the summer.

Along with wild water cress and the hearts of the cattails we gathered along the springs, we had enough nourishment to continue the journey.

Within the cliffs above the Escalante River, we found Moki Indian dwellings, abandoned for some reason, years before. Pottery chards, old matting made of reeds and dry corn cobs were there, untouched.

Many times at night, the sun heated walls of the canyons would cool and exfoliate slabs of sandstone down the cliffs to the canyons below, creating a roar that echoed and re-echoed through the night. It was a bit unnerving! We sought rest and protection under the rock overhangs along the canyon walls.

Eventually we were able to make our way out to the spectacular Boulder Valley, where the early Mormon setters established a remote community, nourished by the clear waters of Boulder Creek. The creek was fed from the snows of the highest forested plateau in the world, Boulder Mountain. My partner, Jim Dyer, had enough. Eventually he made his way back to Escalante and home on his bicycle.

I stayed on with the Doyle Mossman family. Doyle needed a hand to gather and milk twenty-seven cows each morning. The milk was picked up by the local cheese factory, turned into blocks of cheese and packed out by mules over a primitive mountain trail to Escalante for market. Hay was cut and stacked for the herd. It was hard work, work that began at four in the morning, and lasted until dark. My reward was three farm meals a day.

Near the end of August, I traded Doyle my rifle for a horse and saddle. This reliable and steady black horse was named Moki, after the historic Indians that had first settled the area. Doyle then helped me catch a wild horse on Wild Horse Mesa, a mesa later made famous in a book written by Zane Grey. The little mustang was a fighter. I called him Utah, because his roan color was the hue of the land I had learned to love. Eventually, Utah, my new little friend, took to me and became at ease with the pack-saddle.

I shall never forget the brilliant morning I left my Boulder Valley friends and started with the horses over the old Mormon trail to our family ranch in California. A vast and stone-rutted landscape stretched before us. Over a hundred miles to the southeast, across the Colorado River and Arizona, loomed Navajo Mountain. To the west lay the isolated peaks of the San Juan Mountains that jutted to the blue sky. And to the north was the 11,000 foot alpine wilderness of Aquarius plateau and Boulder Mountain. Between these spectacular guideposts were the rugged, red, torn and eroded canyons of rock, which over fifty years later would become the Escalante National Monument. In all this spectacular beauty I was alone and exuberant. My return to California was the horseback ride of a lifetime.

NATURAL AMPHITHEATRE
Escalante River, Utah

"The shear walls of red rock towered along our way. We found massive amphitheaters, carved over the centuries by the flowing water, in which to make our camps. In a sense, we were prisoners within the impenetrable walls of the canyon."

(For perspective, find W. Robinson with his pack on his back. He is climbing a cliff above the river to find sanctuary from storm and foliating slabs of sandstone, in an amphitheater.)

MOKI INDIAN CLIFF DWELLER SITE
Escalante River, Utah

W. Robinson exploring one of the many ruins/sites built in the cliffs above the River.

"Willard Robinson and James Dyer are exploring a little known region of the United States, identified as the Escalante Escarpment. Purpose of the trip is to examine the geological and animal life of the canyon-torn areas, with hope of finding relics left by the Moki Indians, who centuries ago lived in the canyon cliffs of this remote and seldom explored area."

Long Beach Press-Telegram

THE FALLS OF DEATH HOLLOW CANYON
A Tributary of the Escalante River
Escalante, Utah

We tried to find our way out of Escalante Canyon by turning up a tributary known as Death Hollow. We thought this would eventually take us to the little Mormon settlement of Boulder, Utah.

Often our way was so narrow one could reach out and touch both sides of the canyon. In other places the gorge widened enough for river plants to grow. But always the sheer cliffs rose hundreds of feet above.

Six days later we found ourselves trapped and out of food. A sheer wall of cascading water blocked our way.

THE ALASKAN ADVENTURE
1939 – 1940

In the summer of 1939, in search for adventure, my high school friend, Jim Dyer and I left Seattle, Washington in an eighteen-foot sail boat for the Territory of Alaska. It was an adventure! Later, Jim Dyer wrote in a feature article for <u>The Alaska Sportsman</u> magazine:

<u>Recipe for Adventure</u> Take two eager young nomads, a sailboat and the "Inside Passage" to Alaska. Mix well, add a dash of butter, a dash of sweet, and lots of spice! It was such a dish that my friend Willard Robinson and I contemplated hungrily as we cast off our mooring line at Seattle early one June morning in 1939 and turned the bow of our auxiliary powered sloop, the Little Snark, named after Jack London's ship, to the north and Alaska.

We did complete the six week journey to Ketchikan, Alaska, but not without navigational errors, storms, engine failures, treacherous tides, failing winds, and the shortcomings of inexperienced seamen. It was not an adventure for the faint of heart.

Jim Dyer decided to stay on in Ketchikan, joined the U.S. Coast Guard, and spent World War II maintaining the navigational aids along the Alaskan waterways. I traveled on north and enrolled at the University of Alaska in Fairbanks. For me, it was a timely and important decision. Judge Bunnell, the President of the University, gave me a job to cover my expenses, and I was selected as one of twenty to participate in the University of Alaska flight training program. This led to a Commercial Pilot rating, a chance to fly the Alaskan sky--a valued stepping stone to eventually becoming a U. S. Navy Pilot. The details of this period of my life are chronicled in the book, <u>Navy Wings of Gold.</u>

F. Willard Robinson

CRUISE OF THE LITTLE SNARK
August 1939

The "Little Snark" (an 18-foot sloop) on which we made
our trip from Seattle to Alaska.

FAIRBANKS, ALASKA ON A MID-WINTER DAY

Top photo: NYL, EN PHOTOS, Fairbanks, Alaska, 1939

December 21, 1939. Time-lapse photo shows the sun at 15-minute intervals: 10:15 am to 1:00 pm.

Right photo:

Main Entrance (above) to the University of Alaska. The girl's dorm is on the left and the senior men's dorm is on the right. This is where Robinson lived for a year.

Left photo:
Here Robbie dresses native.

"In September 1939, I enrolled as a student at the University of Alaska."

F. Willard Robinson

(Pictures from Navy Wings of Gold, Second Edition, p. 20)

195

FLYING IN ALASKA

"In June, 1940, I became the first United States government-trained, certificated pilot in the Territory of Alaska. It was a high honor and an event that was newsworthy. KFAR, the local radio station in Fairbanks, broadcast my final flight check throughout the Territory."
F. Willard Robinson

Left to right:
F. Willard Robinson, pilot
Bud Foster, NBC announcer
Mr. Gentry, CAA official
Lt. Dick Ragle, instructor

Ski-equipped planes for winter travel at the Fairbanks Airport.

(Pictures from Navy Wings of Gold, Second Edition, p. 21)

F. WILLARD ROBINSON
Chena Slough, Fairbanks, Alaska
August 1940

Noel Wien bought three Fairchild 71's and brought
this one to Fairbanks in 1940. From this beginning
emerged Alaska Airlines.

WORLD WAR II
December 8, 1941 – August 14, 1945

The World War II generation experienced more technical and social change than any other generation in history. From World War I, when the United States matured as a world power, to a few years later when the trauma, upheaval and sheer despair of the Great Depression hit, the people struggled for equilibrium. Unprepared, this generation was called to fight for the preservation of America's freedom; a freedom being challenged by dictatorial powers that sought control of the world. Men and women imbued with patriotism and courage, embarking from their foundation of traditional values, went out to meet the enemy. Along with the pain, suffering and loss, an element of adventure, a community of purpose, optimism and discipline were all carried to the engagement. The men of the Robinson family, three brothers and a brother-in-law, were not exceptions. The three brothers joined the U.S. Navy and the brother-in-law chose the U.S. Marines. December 8, 1941, was when I enlisted.

Within nine months I became a U.S. Navy torpedo and bomber aircraft carrier pilot. Flying the 2,000 horsepower Grumman *Avenger,* as a member of Squadron VC-7, we proudly flew our new war machines to the awaiting aircraft carrier, *Manila Bay.* With precision the squadron dropped from the sky, each pilot establishing his landing interval, then in turn being directed by the Landing Signal Officer to the arresting cable hook on the rolling flight deck of the ship. We were on our way for combat with the Japanese Empire in the far Pacific.

The weeks that followed became a defining period of my life, as later recorded in the book, Navy Wings of Gold.

F. Willard Robinson

F. WILLARD ROBINSON LIEUTENANT, UNITED STATES NAVAL RESERVE

Torpedo Squadron VC-7

United States Naval Air Station

Corpus Christi, Texas

Know all men by these presents that

Ensign Franklin W. Robinson, Jr., A-V(N), USNR

has completed the prescribed course of training, and having met successfully the requirements of the course, has been designated a

Naval Aviator

In Witness Whereof, this certificate has been signed on this 6th day of November 1942, and the Seal of the Naval Air Station, hereunto affixed

Rear Admiral, U. S. Navy
Commandant

Commander, U. S. Navy
Superintendent of Aviation Training

(From Navy Wings of Gold, Second Edition, p. 65)

F.W. ROBINSON JR., NAVAL AVIATOR

Commissioned Ensign USNR
Corpus Christi, Texas
1942
(Pictures from <u>Navy Wings of Gold</u>, Second Edition, p. 64)

THE "JO-DO"
With Plane Captain Stella (Chief Mechanic)
and Lt. F.W.Robinson

Squadron VC-31 photo

"Jo-Do," a TBM Grumman *Avenger* Torpedo Bomber, at the North Island Naval Air Station, San Diego, California. This plane, flown by F.W. Robinson, was the first aircraft in military history to launch air-to-ground missiles. The launch was made on December 3, 1943, flying from the Naval Auxiliary Air Station, Inyokern, California.

(Pictures from <u>Navy Wings of Gold</u>, Second Edition, p. 94)

Ready to Test Fire First Air-to-Ground Missiles
Inyokern Auxiliary Naval Air Station
Inyokern, California
December 3, 1943

Official photo, Squadron VC-7

Lt. Franklin W. Robinson Jr. USNR
in the cockpit of his TBM *Avenger* test plane.
Navy Torpedo and Bombing Squadron VC-7

United States Forces Attack
Marshall Islands

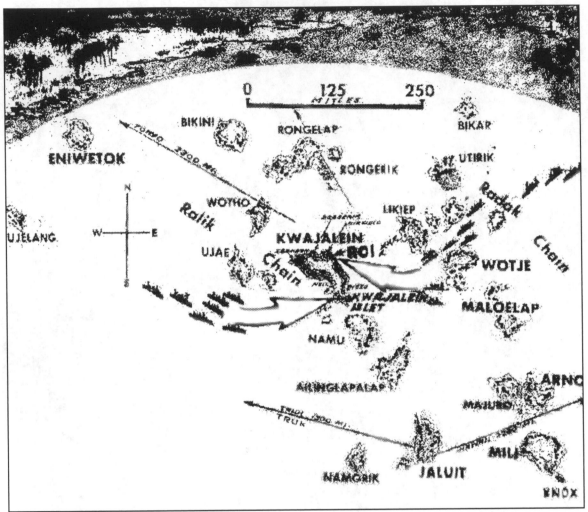

This map and the article below are taken from a 1944 newspaper describing the U.S. Naval attack on the Marshall Islands.

Most Powerful Naval Striking Force in Sea History Leads Attack

PEARL HARBOR, Feb. 1944 (UP) – United States Marine and Army troops, supported by the most powerful naval striking force in history, have battled ashore on Kwajalein atoll in the Marshall Islands and won firm beach heads near Roi and Kwajalein inlets in a successful opening of the greatest combined operation of the Pacific war, it was announced.

Clouds of planes and new secret weapons hitherto unused in war also supported the troops as they splashed across the coral reefs in their first onslaught.   *(Pictures from <u>Navy Wings of Gold</u>, Second Edition, p. 132)*

U.S. NAVY AIRCRAFT CARRIER
SQUADRON VC-7

Lt. Franklin W. Robinson Jr.
Leading Section of TBM *Avenger* Torpedo Bombers
December 1943

NOTE: The "new secret weapons hitherto unused in war" referred to in the United Press release (previous page) regarding the attack on the Marshall Islands, pertains to the air-to-ground rockets fired from the TBM Grumman *Avengers* by the pilots of Navy Flight Squadron VC-7, flying from the deck of the escort carrier *USS Manila Bay*.

(Pictures from <u>Navy Wings of Gold</u>, Second Edition, p. 133)

BEVERLY HILLS HIGH SCHOOL
1962

Leadership for a Revitalized High School Program
F. Willard Robinson, Ed.D., Principal

Beverly Hills High School, in providing the most meaningful educational program for students, has accepted the need for more flexibility in curriculum experiences and program scheduling. The adoption of the concept of a more flexible school program carries with it a commitment to alter nearly every aspect of school operation. Curriculum content, teaching methods, instructional material, class organization, school structure, teacher preparation, school staffing—all must be perceived in varying patterns that enable the flexibility required.

With this in mind, we have developed a new and remodeled school plant, provided workshops to enable planning and preparation of staff, employed specialized personnel, and developed a basic plan to phase-in the new program. We must meet the basic educational challenges of our day.

F. Willard Robinson

BEVERLY HILLS PRINCIPAL
A Personal Story of Leadership in the Tumultuous 1960's

. . . .there was a "Happening" at the Flagpole.

This is the story of a man who, like his pioneer forbearers, reached for his own frontiers in educational leadership during the historic time of the 1960's when the cultural foundations of America were challenged by rebellious young people. "Take over," the dissidents yelled, "and we can control any high school in the nation." It all came to a climax at the *"Happening"* at the Beverly Hill High School flagpole.

The book, <u>Beverly Hills Principal</u>, is a love story between a man in conflict and his faithful wife. Together they move through the turmoil of global war, illness, uncertainty, conflict and growth. Their loyalty, support, commitment to one another, and above all their deep spiritual faith, will sustain them.

(Beverly Hills Principal was first published by Writers Press of Boise, Idaho, ©1999 F. Willard Robinson, Ed. D.)

JOAN and F. WILLARD ROBINSON

Sixty-fourth Wedding Anniversary Picture – Boise, Idaho, 2007

"Now, after sixty-four years of marriage, Robbie and I look back on a rich and eventful life; a life full of blessings beyond our greatest dreams. The challenges we have faced over the years have been formative. It is possible to say that the events, both bad and good, have permanently molded our souls and our character. Even the bad times helped in putting us on a path of faith and courage, which has sustained us to this day. We have been blessed."

Joan Robinson

Congressional Record

PROCEEDINGS AND DEBATES OF THE 94th CONGRESS, FIRST SESSION

United States of America

Vol. 121 — WASHINGTON, TUESDAY, DECEMBER 2, 1975 — *No. 176*

House of Representatives

TRIBUTE TO DR. F. WILLARD ROBINSON

HON. THOMAS M. REES
OF CALIFORNIA
IN THE HOUSE OF REPRESENTATIVES
Tuesday, December 2, 1975

Mr. REES. Mr. Speaker, I am proud today to call to the attention of my colleagues in Congress the name and the achievements of Dr. F. Willard Robinson.

Dr. Robinson is a man who has devoted his life to the service of others, particularly the youth of our Nation.

His early years were spent in his own education, at Long Beach Polytechnic High School and at the University of Southern California. He achieved high scholastic honors and also distinguished himself on the debating team and on the track and cross-country teams.

As was the case with so many others, Willard Robinson's education was interrupted by World War II. He defended his country as a pilot in a carrier-based torpedo squadron, operating in the Pacific area. He served 54 months active duty as lieutenant in naval aviation.

After the war, Willard Robinson returned to the University of Southern California for graduate work in education, to better equip himself for the teaching of young people. He earned the M.S. and Ed. D. degrees in education as well as secondary and general administrative credentials.

Dr. Robinson has contributed to the educational process and the educational systems of the State of California and the United States in many ways. He has worked without respite in the California and National Associations of Secondary School Administrators. He was also a Director of the College Entrance Examination Board.

Since 1959, Dr. Robinson has concentrated most of his efforts at Beverly Hills High School where he has directed and supervised the development of an educational program without equal. He has provided the kind of leadership that has resulted in the steady improvement and broadening of programs to meet the needs of the students through the most difficult period in the history of education in our country.

The strength of a man is permanently etched against the background of his accomplishments. This man's courage has borne him through military fire and pioneer flight to the forefront of education. Nurtured in the heritage of stern religious forebears, a man displays his power to grow as he bends with the times. To change from strict traditionalism to open, people-oriented leadership is a measure of a man's sensitivity and involvement with the future. Climaxing a life with a third career routed in idealism and dedicated to building models for today's youth is the pinnacle of achievement. Willard Robinson is such a man, a unique human being of talent and integrity.

I ask the House of Representatives to join me in saluting an outstanding American, F. Willard Robinson.

I don't know . . .

What I do know ...

Life is a gift and a mystery.

Discovering the lives of our ancestors brings reward.

Our forbearer's sought first the Kingdom of God.

Faithfulness to the assured theological hope of the eternal sustained them through the vicissitudes of life.

We are blessed by their faith, heroism and example.

F. Willard Robinson
September 11, 2007
Age 89

Printed in the United States
by Baker & Taylor Publisher Services